MW01533048

Talee

www.talee.org

Copyright @ 2014 Talee All rights reserved

This book is one of the many Islamic publications distributed by Talee throughout the world in different languages with the aim of conveying the message of Islam to the people of the world. Talee (www.talee.org) is a registered Organization that operates and is sustained through collaborative efforts of volunteers in many countries around the world, and it welcomes your involvement and support. Its objectives are numerous, yet its main goal is to spread the truth about the Islamic faith in general and the Shi`a School of Thought in particular due to the latter being misrepresented, misunderstood and its tenets often assaulted by many ignorant folks, Muslims and non-Muslims. Organization's purpose is to facilitate the dissemination of knowledge through a global medium, the Internet, to locations where such resources are not commonly or easily accessible or are resented, resisted and fought! In addition, Talee aims at encouraging scholarship, research and enquiry through the use of technological facilitates.

For a complete list of our published books please refer to our website (www.talee.org) or send us an email to info@talee.org

LIGHT
WITHIN ME

Ayatullah Murtada Mutahhari
Allamah Muhammad Husayn Tabatabai
Ayatullah Ruhullah Khumayni

XKP

Chapter 1

Preface - Allamah Husayn Tabatabai

Allamah Muhammad Husayn Tabatabai

Although most people are preoccupied with earning their livelihood and pay little attention to spiritual matters, yet every man has an inherent desire to know the absolute truth. When this dormant power comes to surface and is awakened in some people, they gain a number of spiritual perceptions.

Despite the claim of the sophists and the atheists that every truth is an illusion, everybody believes in the existence of one eternal truth. When man with a pure heart and a pure spirit looks at the permanent factuality of the universe and at the same time observes the instability and transience of its various parts, he realizes that this world and its manifestations are a mirror which reflects the existence of one eternal truth. With this realization his joy knows no bounds and he is so elated that in his eyes everything else becomes insignificant and worthless.

This spectacle forms the basis of that impulse of the gnostics1 which draws the attention of the godly people to a world beyond perception and cultivates the love of Allah in their hearts. The pull which they feel towards this spectacle makes them forget everything and removes many desires from their hearts. This pull leads man to the worship of the Invisible Being who is more manifest than all that is visible or audible. It is this pull which gave birth to many a religion based on Allah's worship. The real gnostic is he who worships Allah not, because he hopes for any reward or is afraid of any punishment, but only because he knows Him and loves Him.2

It is clear from the above that gnosis is not a religion like other religions. It is to be regarded as the central and the most vital part of all religions. Gnosis is a perfect way of worship, based on love, not on fear or hope. It is a way of understanding the inner facts of religion instead of being contented with its outward and perceptible form. Among the followers of all revealed religions, even among those who believe in idol-worship there are individuals who follow the path of gnosis. The gnostics are found among the followers of polytheistic religions3 as well as among the Jews, Christians, Zoroastrians and Muslims.

Appearance of Gnosis in Islam

Out of the companions of the Holy Prophet Imam Ali is known for the eloquent description of gnostic truths and the stages of spiritual life. His sayings on this subject are a treasure of knowledge. As for the other companions of the Holy Prophet, their sayings which have come down to us do not contain enough material on this subject. The majority of the mystics and gnostics, whether Sunni or Shi'ah consider the chain of their spiritual leaders going to Imam Ali through such companions of his as Salman Farsi, Uways Qarani, Kumayl bin Ziyad, Rashid Hujari, Mitham Tammar, Rabi' bin Khaytham and Hasan Basri.

Next to this group some other persons like Taus Yamani, Shayban Ra'i, Malik ibn Dinar, Ibrahim bin Adham and Sharif Balkhi appeared in the second century, They were considered holy men by the people. These persons were apparently ascetics. They did not talk openly of gnosis or mysticism, though they conceded that they were introduced to spiritualism by the first group and trained by it.

Towards the end of the second century and the beginning of the third some other individuals like Bayazid Bistami, Ma'ruf Karkhi and Junayd Baghdadi appeared. They openly talked of gnosis. Some of their esoteric sayings based on their spiritual intuition were apparently so obnoxious that they were strongly denounced and condemned by some jurists and theologians. Consequently several of these gnostics were imprisoned and flogged and a few of them were even put to death.4 Nevertheless this group continued to flourish and maintained its activities despite all opposition. Thus the development of gnosis or mysticism continued till this system reached the zenith of its popularity and expansion in the seventh and the eighth centuries. During the later periods its popularity fluctuated from time to time, but it has been able to maintain its existence in the Islamic world till today.

It appears that most of the mystic leaders whose names are found in biographies and memoirs belonged to the Sunni school of thought and the current Sufi system that comprises some ceremonials and rituals not consistent with the teachings of the Qur'an and Sunnah, is the heritage transmitted by these gnostics and mystics, although their system has subsequently adopted a few Shi'ah rites also.

Some spiritual leaders hold that no mystic or gnostic system or programme was prescribed by Islam. The present gnostic system was invented by the mystics themselves; yet it has the approbation of Allah in the same way as monasticism was sanctioned by Allah after it had been introduced by the Christians into their religion with a view to propagate Christianity.

Anyway the mystics trace the chain of their spiritual leaders to Imam Ali through their early preceptors. (This chain of spiritual descent resembles a genealogical tree). The account of the visions and intuitions of the early gnostics also which has come down to us, mostly contains those elements of spiritual life which we find in the sayings, and teachings of Imam Ali and other Imams of the Holy Prophet's Household (Ahlul Bayt). We can clearly observe these facts provided we study their (the mystics) teachings patiently and calmly and are not carried away by their fascinating sayings which are often obnoxious and blasphemous.

(i) The sufis (Muslim mystics) regard the holiness acquired by following the spiritual path as human perfection. According to the Shi'ah belief, this quality is possessed by the Imams5 and through them can be acquired by their true followers.

(ii) The sufi doctrine that there must always be a Qutb6 in the world and the qualities they attribute to him, correspond to the Shi'ah doctrine of Imamat. According to the "People of the Holy Prophet's Household" the Imam (in Sufi terminology the perfect man) is a manifestation of Allah's Names7 and is responsible for supervising and guiding all human activities. This being the Shi'ah conception of Wilayat, the great Sufis may be regarded as the proponents of the Shi'ah doctrine, though apparently they followed the Sunni school. What we mean to say is that the Shi'ites being the followers of an infallible Imam, already possess all that is indicated by the mystics. As a matter of fact the Qutb or the perfect man conceived by the mystics does not actually exist anywhere outside the Shi'ite world. Mere presumption is obviously quite a different thing.

It may be mentioned here that some authentic Sunni books state that the outward form of the Islamic law and Islamic teachings does not explain how to perform spiritual journey.8 On this basis the Sufis say that they have individually discovered certain methods and ways which facilitate this journey. They also claim that their methods have gained Divine sanction in the same way as previously monasticism had gained.9 As such the Sufi leaders included in their programme of spiritual journey whatever rites, rituals and formalities they deemed fit, and asked their disciples to observe them. Gradually a vast and independent system came into being. This system included such items as total obedience, liturgy, special robes, music and ecstasy and rapture at the time of repeating the liturgical formulas. Some orders of the Sufis went to the extent of separating the tariqah (the Sufi way) from the shari'ah (Islamic precepts). The adherents of these Sufi orders practically joined hands with the Batinites (Those who believe that in Islam everything is allegorical and has a hidden meaning). Anyhow according to the Shi'ah point of view the original source, of Islam, namely the Qur'an and Sunnah indicate what is absolutely contrary to all this. It is not possible that the religious texts would not guide to the truth or would ignore to explain an essential programme. Nor is anybody, whosoever, he may be, allowed to ignore his duty in regard to what is obligatory or is prohibited according to the injunctions of Islam.

What do the Qur'an and Sunnah say about Gnosis?

At a number of places in the Holy Qur'an Allah has directed people to ponder over the contents of the Holy Book and not to pass by them cursorily. In a large number of verses, the universe and the entire creation have been described as Allah's signs. They have been called so because they indicate a great truth. When a man sees red light as a sign of danger, his attention is concentrated on the danger and he ceases to pay attention to the light itself. If he still thinks of the shape, colour and nature of light, then these things will absorb his attention and he will not he able to attend to the impending danger. Similarly the universe and its manifestations are the signs of their Creator, an evidence of His existence and His power. They have no independent existence. We may look at them from any aspect, they indicate nothing but Allah. He who looks at the world and the people of the world from this angle under the guidance of the Qur'an, he will perceive Allah alone. He will not be fascinated by the borrowed charms of this world, but will see an infinite Beauty, a Beloved manifesting Himself from behind the curtain of this world. No doubt, as we have explained by citing the example of red light, what the signs indicate is not this world, but the person of its Creator. We may say that the relationship between Allah and this world is not that of 1 + 1 or 1 x 1, but is that of 1 + 0. In other words, this world in relation to Allah is a nonentity and does not add anything to His Essence.

As soon as man realizes this fact, his notion of having an independent existence is smashed and he suddenly feels imbibed with love of Allah. Obviously this realization does not come through eyes, ears or any other sensory organs or mental faculties, for all organs themselves are mere signs and cannot play any significant role in providing the guidance we are talking about.10

When a man having access to Divine manifestation and desiring to re-member Allah alone, hears the following passage of the Qur'an, he comes to know that the only path of perfect guidance is that of knowing himself:

O you who believe, you have charge of your own souls. He who errs cannot injure you if you are rightly guided. (al-Ma'idah, 5:105)

He understands that his true guide is Allah alone who enjoins upon him to know himself and to seek the path of self-knowing, leaving all other paths. He must see Allah through the window of his own soul and thus achieve his real objective. That is why the Holy Prophet has said: He who has known himself, has known Allah.11

He has also said: "Those of you who know Allah better, better they know themselves."12

As for the embarking on spiritual journey there are many verses of the Qur'an which urge the people to remember Allah. For example at one place the Qur'an says: Remember Me, I will remember you. (al-Baqarah, 2:152)

Man has been ordered to do good deeds also, which have been explained in the Qur'an and the Sunnah. Mentioning the good deeds Allah says: Surely in the Messenger of Allah you have a good example. (al-Ahzab, 33:21)

How can it be imagined that Islam would declare that there was a path leading towards Allah without appraising the people what that path is?

And how can it be that Allah would mention a path without explaining how it is to be traversed?

Allah says in the Holy Qur'an: Messenger, We have revealed this Book to you. It contains the details of everything. (Surah an-Nahl, 16:89)

Notes:

The Islamic esoterics known as Irfan or gnosis is sometimes associated with Tasawwuf or mysticism whose certain rites and rituals are repugnant to Islam. However Shi'aism considers Islamic acts of worship to be sufficient for gaining proximity to Allah.

Imam Ja'far Sadiq has said: "There are three categories of the worshippers: 'Those who worship Allah out of fear; their worship is that of the slaves. Those who worship Allah for the sake of a reward; their worship is that of the wage-earners. Those who worship Allah out of love and earnestness; their worship is that of the freeman. This last is the best form of worship." (Biharul Anwar, vol. V, p. 208).

Here the learned author has in his mind the religions of India and the Far

East in which different aspects of divinity are represented by gods and godesses in a mythical and symbolic form.

Refer to the books on the biographies of the sages, such as the Tazkiratul Awliya' by Attar and the Taraiqul Haqa'iq by Ma'sum 'Ali Shah.

The twelve successors explicitly expressed by the Holy Prophet of Islam through Divine Will.

When a gnostic becomes totally oblivious of himself, in the Sufi parlance, he is said to have passed away in God, for he completely surrenders himself to the will and guidance of Allah.

The gnostics maintain that the world has derived its entity from the Names of Allah and its existence and continuity depend on them. The source of Allah's all Names is His most perfect and loftiest Name. This Name is the station of the perfect man, called the Qutb of the universe also. The world is never without a Qutb.

In Islam spiritual journey is called Sair wa Suluk, which signifies a journey towards Allah.

Allah says: But monkery the Chnstian invented, We ordained it not for them. We ordained only seeking Allah's pleasure, but they observed it not. (Surah al-Hadid, 57:27).

Imam Ali has said: "Allah is not that who may be comprehended by knowledge. Allah is He Who guides the argument to Himself." (Biharul Anwar, vol. II p. 186).

A well-known tradition repeatedly quoted in the books of both the Sunni and Shi'ah gnostics.

Another tradition cited in the books of the Sunni and Shi'ah gnostics.

Chapter 2

Part 1: by Shaheed Murtada Mutahhari - An Introduction to Irfan

Shaheed Murtada Mutahhari

This short introduction to irfan is a part of the author's book Ashnai ba ulum e Islami (An Introduction to the Islamic Sciences) written in seven parts, 1) logic, 2) philosophy, 3) kalam, 4) irfan, 5) fiqh, 6) usul al fiqh, 7) hikmat e amali (ethics).

'Irfan is one of the disciplines that originated within the realm of Islamic culture and developed there to attain a high level of sophistication. But before we can begin to discuss 'irfan, we must realize that it can be approached from two viewpoints: the social and the academic. Unlike the scholars of other Islamic disciplines - such as the Quranic commentators (mufassirun), the scholars of hadith (muhaddithun), the jurisprudents (fuqaha'), the theologians (mutakallimun), the philosophers, the men of literature, and the poets - the 'urafa' are a group of scholars who have not only developed their own science, 'irfan, producing great scholars and important books, but have also given rise within the Islamic world to a distinct social grouping. In this the 'urafa' are unique; for the scholars of the other Islamic disciplines - such as the jurisprudents, for instance - form solely academic groupings and are not viewed as a social group distinct from the rest of society.

In view of this distinction the gnostics, when referred to as belonging to a certain academic discipline, are called 'urafa' and when referred to as a social group are generally called Sufis (mutasawwifah).

The 'urafa' and sufis are not regarded as forming a separate sect in Islam, nor do they claim themselves to be such. They are to be found within every Islamic school and sect, yet, at the same time, they coalesce to form a distinct social group. The factors that set them apart from the rest of

Islamic society are a distinctive chain of ideas and opinions, a special code governing their social intercourse, dress and even, sometimes, the way they wear their hair and beards, and their living communally in their hospices. (Pers. Khaniqah; Ar-ribat, zawiyah; Turk. tekkiye)

Of course, there are and have always been 'urafa' - particularly amongst the Shi'ah - who bear none of these external signs to distinguish them socially from others; yet, at the same time, they have been profoundly involved in the spiritual methodology of 'irfan (sayr wa suluk). It is these who are the real gnostics; not those who have invented for themselves hundreds of special mannerisms and customs and have brought innovations into being.

In this series of lectures, in which we are taking a general look at Islamic sciences and disciplines, we will not be dealing with the social and sectarian aspect of gnosis, that is to say, tasawwuf (sufism). We will limit ourselves to an examination of 'irfan as a discipline and branch amongst the branches of Islam's scientific culture. To look thoroughly at the social aspects of sufism would require us to examine its causes and origins, the effects - positive and negative, beneficial and detrimental - it has and has had upon Islamic society, the nature of the relations between the sufis and other Islamic groups, the hue it has given to the whole of Islamic teachings, and the role it has played in the diffusion of Islam throughout the world. This is far beyond the range of these lectures, and here we will consider the tradition of 'irfan only as a science and as one of the academic disciplines of Islam.

'Irfan, as a scientific and academic discipline, itself has two branches: the practical and the theoretical. The practical aspect of 'irfan describes and explains the relationship and responsibilities the human being bears towards itself, towards the world and towards God. Here, 'irfan is similar to ethics (akhlaq), both of them being practical sciences. There do exist differences, however, and later we will explain them.

The practical teaching of 'irfan is also called the itinerary of the spiritual path (sayr wa suluk; lit. 'traveling and journeying'). Here, the wayfarer (salik) who desires to reach the goal of the sublime peak of humanness - that is to say, tawhid - is told where to set off, the ordered stages and stations that he must traverse, the states and conditions he will undergo at these stations, and the events that will befall him. Needless to say, all these stages and stations must be passed under the guidance and supervision of a mature and perfect example of humanity who, having traveled this path, is aware of the manners and ways of each station. If not, and there is no perfect human being to guide him on his path, he is in danger of going astray.

The perfect man, the master, who must necessarily accompany the novice on the spiritual journey according to the 'urafa', has been called in their vocabulary as Ta'ir al-quds (the Holy Bird) and Khidr:
Accompany my zeal on the path, O Ta'ir al-Quds, The path to the goal is long, and I new to the journey. Leave not this stage without the company of Khidr, There is darkness ahead; be afraid of losing the way. Of course, there is a world of difference between the tawhid of the 'arif and the general view of tawhid. For the 'arif, tawhid is the sublime peak of humanness and the final goal of his spiritual journey, while for the ordinary people, and even the philosophers, tawhid means the essential Unity of the Necessary Being. For the 'arif, tawhid means that the ultimate reality is only God, and everything other than God is mere appearance, not reality. The 'arif's tawhid means that 'other than God there is nothing'. For the 'arif, tawhid means following a path and arriving at the stage when he sees nothing but God. However, this view of tawhid is not accepted by the opponents of the 'urafa', and some of them have declared such a view to be heretic. Yet the 'urafa' are convinced that this is the only true tawhid, and that the other stages of it cannot be said to be free of polytheism (shirk).

The 'urafa' do not see the attainment of the ideal stage of tawhid to be the function of reason and reflection. Rather they consider it to be the work of the heart, and attained through struggle, through the journeying, and through purifying and disciplining the self.

This, however, is the practical aspect of 'irfan, which is not unlike ethics in this respect, for both discuss a series of things that 'ought to be done'. However, there are differences, and the first of these is that 'irfan discusses the human being's relationship with itself, with the world and with God, and its primal concern is man's relationship with God. Systems of ethics, on the other hand, do not all consider it necessary for the relationship between man and God to be discussed; it is only the religious ethical systems that give importance and attention to this matter.

The second difference is that the methodology of spiritual progression, sayr wa suluk, as the words sayr (traveling) and suluk (journeying) imply, is a dynamic one, while ethics is static. That is, 'irfan speaks about a point of departure, a destination, and the stages and stations which, in their correct order, the wayfarer must traverse in order to arrive at the final destination. In the 'arif's view, there really is a path before the human being - a path that is actual and not in the least a metaphor - and this path must be followed stage by stage, station by station; to arrive at any station without having traversed the preceding one is, in the 'arif's view, impossible. Thus the 'arif views the human soul to be a living organism, like a seedling or like a child, whose perfection lies in growth and maturation in accordance with a particular system and order.

In ethics, however, the subjects are handled solely as a series of virtues, such as righteousness, honesty, sincerity, chastity, generosity, justice, and preferring others over oneself (ithar), to name but a few, with which the soul must be adorned. In the view of ethics, the human soul is rather like a house to be furnished with a series of beautiful objects, pictures and decorations, and no importance is attached to a particular sequence. It is not important where one begins or where one ends. It is of no consequence whether one starts at the ceiling or at the walls, at the top of a wall or at the bottom and so on. On the contrary, in 'irfan the ethical elements are discussed in a dynamic perspective.

The third difference between these two disciplines is that the spiritual elements of ethics are limited to concepts and ideas that are generally commonplace, while the spiritual elements of 'irfan are much more profound and expansive. In the spiritual methodology of 'irfan, much mention is made of the heart and the states and happenings it will experience, and these experiences are known only to the wayfarer of the path during the course of his struggles and his journey on the path, while other people have no idea of these states and happenings.

The other branch of 'irfan is related to interpretation of being, that is, God, the universe, and the human being. Here 'irfan resembles philosophy, for both seek to understand existence, whereas practical 'irfan seeks, like ethics, to change the human being. However, just as there are differences between practical 'irfan and ethics, so also there exist differences between theoretical 'irfan and philosophy, and in the following section we will explain these differences.

Theoretical Irfan:
Theoretical 'irfan, as said before, is concerned with ontology, and

علم الوجود

11

discusses God, the world, and the human being. This aspect of 'irfan resembles theological philosophy (falsafeh-ye ilahi), which also seeks to describe being. Like theological philosophy, 'irfan also defines its subject, essential principles and problems, but whereas philosophy relies solely upon rational principles for its arguments, 'irfan bases its deductions on principles discovered through mystic experience (kashf) and then reverts to the language of reason to explain them.

The rationalistic deductions of philosophy can be likened to studying a passage written originally in the same language; the arguments of 'irfan, on the other hand, are like studying something that has been translated from some other language in which it was originally written. To be more precise, the 'arif wishes to explain those things which he claims to have witnessed with his heart and his entire being by using the language of reason.

The ontology of 'irfan is in several ways profoundly different from the ontology of philosophers. In the philosopher's view, both God and other things have reality, with the difference that while God is the Necessary Being (wajib al-wujud) and Existing-By-Himself, things other than God are only possible existents (mumkin al-wujud), existing-through-another, and are effects of the Necessary Being. However, the 'arif's ontology has no place for things other than God as existing alongside Him, even if they are effects of which He is the cause; rather, the Divine Being embraces and encompasses all things. That is to say, all things are names, qualities, and manifestations of God, not existents alongside Him.

The aim of the philosopher also differs from that of the 'arif. The philosopher wishes to understand the world; he wishes to form in his mind a correct and relatively complete picture of the realm of existence. The philosopher considers the highest mark of human perfection to lie in perceiving, by way of reason, the exact nature of existence, so that the macrocosm finds a reflection within his mind while he in turn becomes a rational microcosm. Thus it is said when defining philosophy that: [Philosophy is] the (final) development of a rational knower ('alim) into an actual world ('alam).

This means that philosophy is a study whereby a human being becomes a rational microcosm similar to the actual macrocosm. But the 'arif, on the other hand, would have nothing to do with reason and understanding; he wishes to reach the very kernel and reality of existence, God, to become connected to it and witness it.

In the 'arif's view, human perfection does not mean having a picture of the realm of existence in one's mind; rather it is to return, by means of treading the spiritual path of progression, to the origin from which one has come, to overcome the separation of distance between oneself and the Divine Essence, and, in the realm of nearness, to obliterate one's finite self to abide in Divine Infinitude.

The tools of the philosopher are reason, logic and deduction, while the tools of the 'arif are the heart, spiritual struggle, purification and disciplining of the self, and an inner dynamism.

Later, when we come to the world-view of 'irfan, we shall also discuss how it differs from the world-view of philosophy.

'Irfan, both practical and theoretical, is closely connected with the holy religion of Islam. Like every other religion - in fact more than any other religion - Islam has explained the relationships of man with God, with the world, and with himself; and it has also given attention to describing and explaining existence.

Now, the question inevitably arises here about the relation between the ideas of 'irfan and the teachings of Islam. Of course, the 'urafa' never claim that they have something to say that is above or beyond Islam, and they are earnest in their denials of any such imputations. In fact, they claim to have discovered more of the realities of Islam, and that they are the true Muslims. Whether in the practical teaching of 'irfan or the theoretical, the 'urafa' always support their views by referral to the Quran, the Sunnah of the Prophet and the Imams, and the practice of the eminent amongst the Prophet's Companions.

However, others have held different views about the 'urafa', and these may be mentioned:

(a) A group of muhaddithun and jurisprudents has been of the view that the 'urafa' are not practically bound to Islam, and that their referrals to the Quran and the Sunnah are merely a ruse to deceive the simple-minded people and to draw to themselves the hearts of the Muslims. This group is of the view that 'irfan, basically, has no connection with Islam.

(b) A group of modernists who do not have favourable relations with Islam and are ready to give a tumultuous welcome to anything that gives the appearance of freedom from the observances prescribed by the Shari'ah (ibahah) and which can be interpreted as a movement or uprising in the past against Islam and its laws, like the first group, believe that in practice the 'urafa' had no faith or belief in Islam, and that 'irfan and tasawwuf was a movement of the non-Arab peoples against Islam and the Arabs, disguised under the robes of spirituality.

This group and the first are united in their view that the 'urafa' are opposed to Islam. The difference between them is that the first group considers Islam to be sacred and, by banking on the Islamic sentiments of the Muslim masses, wishes to condemn the 'urafa' and, in this way, to hoot them off from the stage of the Islamic sciences. The second group, however, by leaning on the great personalities of the 'urafa'- some of whom are of world-renown - wishes to use them as a means of propaganda against Islam. They detract Islam on the grounds that the subtle and sublime ideas of 'irfan found in Islamic culture are in fact alien to Islam. They consider that these elements entered Islamic culture from outside, for, they say, Islam and its ideas thrive on a far lower level. This group also claims that the 'urafa's citations of the Quran and hadith were solely due to dissimulation and fear of the masses. This, they claim, was a means for them to save their lives.

(c) Besides the above two, there is also a third group which takes a rather neutral view of 'irfan. The view of this group is that 'irfan and sufism contain many innovations and deviations that do not accord with the Quran and the traditions; that this is more true of the practical teaching of 'irfan than its theoretical ideas, especially where it takes a sectarian aspect. Yet, they say, the 'urafa', like the Islamic scholars of other ranks and the majority of Islamic sects, have had the most sincere intentions towards Islam, never wishing to make any assertions contrary to its teachings. It is quite possible that they have made mistakes, in the same way as the other types of scholars - theologians, philosophers, Quranic commentators, and jurisprudents - have made mistakes, but this has never been due to an evil intention towards Islam.

In the view of this group, the issue of the 'urafa's supposed opposition to Islam was raised by those who harbored a special prejudice either against 'irfan or against Islam. If a person were to disinterestedly study the books of the 'urafa', provided that he is acquainted with their terminology and language, although he might come across many a mistake, he will not doubt the sincerity of their complete devotion to Islam.

Of the three views, I prefer the third. I do not believe that the 'urafa' have had evil intentions towards Islam. At the same time I believe that it is necessary for those having specialized knowledge of 'irfan and of the profound teachings of Islam to undertake an objective research and disinterested study of the conformity of the issues of 'irfan with Islamic teachings.

Shari'ah, Tariqah and Haqiqah:

One of the important points of contention between the 'urafa' and the non-'urafa', especially the jurisprudents, is the particular teaching of 'irfan regarding the Shari'ah, the Tariqah (the Way) and the Haqiqah (the Reality). Both agree in saying that the Shari'ah, the body of Islamic laws, is based upon a series of realities and beneficial objectives. The jurisprudents generally interpret these goals to consist of certain things that lead the human being to felicity, that is, to the highest possible level of benefit from God's material and spiritual favors to man. The 'urafa', on the other hand, believe that all the paths end in God, and that all goals and realities are merely the means, causes and agencies that impel the human being towards God.

The jurisprudents say only that underlying the laws of the Shariah is a series of benign objectives, that these objectives constitute the cause and spirit of the Shari'ah, and that the only way of attaining these objectives is to act in accordance with the Shari'ah. But the 'urafa' believe that the realities and objectives underlying the laws of the Shari'ah are of the nature of stations and stages on the human being's ascent towards God and in the process of man's access to the ultimate reality.

The 'urafa' believe that the esoteric*aspect of the Shari'ah is the Way, the Tariqah, at whose end is the Reality (al-Haqiqah), that is tawhid (in the sense mentioned earlier), which is a stage acquired after the obliteration of the 'arif's self and his egoism. Thus the gnostic believes in three things: the Shari'ah, the Tariqah, and the Haqiqah, and that the Shari'ah is the means to, or the shell of the Tariqah, and the Tariqah again is the means to or the shell of the kernel of Haqiqah.

We have explained how the jurisprudents view Islam in the lectures on kalam.[1] They believe that the Islamic teachings can be grouped into three branches. The first of these is kalam, which deals with the principal doctrines (usul al-'aqa'id). In matters related to the doctrines it is necessary for the human being to acquire, through reason, shakeless belief and faith.

The second branch is ethics (akhlaq). It sets forth the instructions about one's duty in regard to ethical virtues and vices.

The third branch, fiqh, deals with the laws (ahkam), which relate to our external actions and behavior.

These three branches of Islamic teachings are separate from each other. The branch of kalam is related to thought and reason; the branch of

15

akhlaq is related to the self, its faculties and habits; and the branch of fiqh is related to the organs and limbs of the body.

However, on the subject of doctrines, the 'urafa' do not consider merely mental and rational belief to be sufficient. They claim that whatever is to be believed in must be arrived at; one must strive to remove the veils between oneself and those realities.

Similarly, with respect to the second branch they do not consider ethics to be adequate on account of its being static and limited. In place of a philosophical ethics, they suggest a spiritual methodology (sayr wa suluk) with its particular composition.

Finally, in the third branch, they have no criticisms; only in specific instances do they express opinions that could, possibly, be taken as being opposed to the laws of fiqh.

These three branches are, therefore, termed by the 'urafa' as Shari'ah, Tariqah, and Haqiqah. Yet they believe that in exactly the same way as the human being cannot be divided into three sections, that is, the body, the self, and reason, which are not separate from each other and form an indivisible whole of which they constitute inward and outward aspects, so it is with the Shari'ah, the Tariqah, and the Haqiqah. One is outward shell, another is inward kernel, and the third is the kernel of the kernel. There is a difference, however, in that the 'urafa' consider the stages of human existence to be more than three; that is, they believe in a stage that transcends the domain of reason. God willing, this shall be explained later.

The Origins of Islamic 'Irfan:

In order to understand any discipline or science, it is essential to study its history and the historical developments associated with it. One must also be acquainted with the personalities who have originated or inherited it and with its source books. In this lecture, and the fourth one, we will turn to these matters.

The first issue to arise is whether Islamic 'irfan is a discipline that originated in the Islamic tradition, such as fiqh, usul al-fiqh, tafsir, and 'ilm al-hadith. That is, is it one of those disciplines that were originated by the Muslims who, having received in Islam the original inspiration, sources and raw material, developed them by discovering their rules and principles? Or is it one of those sciences that found their way into the Islamic world from outside, like medicine and mathematics, which were then developed further by the Muslims in the environment of Islamic civilization and culture? Or is there a third possibility?

The 'urafa' themselves maintain the first of these alternatives, and are in no way ready to admit any other. Some orientalists, however, have insisted - and some still insist - on the second view that 'irfan and its subtle and sublime ideas have come into the Islamic world from outside. Sometimes they maintain a Christian origin for it, and claim that mysticism in Islam is the result of early contact of the Muslims with Christian monks. At other times they claim it to be a result of the Persians' reaction against Islam and the Arabs. Then again sometimes they make it entirely a product of Neo-Platonism, which itself was composed of the ideas of Plato, Aristotle and Pythagoras, influenced by Alexandrian gnosticism and the views and beliefs of Judaism and Christianity. Sometimes they claim it to be derived from Buddhism. Similarly, the opponents of 'irfan in the Islamic world also strive to show the whole of 'irfan and sufism as being alien to Islam, and for this purpose they too maintain that gnosis has non-Islamic origins.

A third view admits that 'irfan, whether practical or theoretical, draws its primary inspiration and material from Islam itself; having taken this material, it has tried to give it a structure by devising certain rules and principles and in this process has also been influenced by external currents, specially the ideas of scholasticism and philosophy, especially of the Illuminationist school. Now there are a number of questions which arise in this context. Firstly, to what extent have the 'urafa' been successful in developing correct rules and principles for structuring their material? Have the 'urafa' been as successful in carrying this out as the jurisprudents? To what extent have the 'urafa' felt themselves bound not to deviate from the actual principles of Islam? And, similarly, to what extent has 'irfan been influenced by the ideas of outside traditions? Has 'irfan assimilated these external ideas by shaping them in its particular moulds, and used them in its development? Or, contrarily, have the waves of these foreign currents carried away 'irfan in their flow?

Each of these questions requires a separate study and careful research. But that which is certain is that 'irfan has derived its basic sources of inspiration from Islam itself and from nowhere else. Let us consider this point.

Those who accept the first view, and to some extent also those who take the second view, see Islam as being a simple religion, popular and unsophisticated, free of all sorts of mysteries and difficult or unintelligible profundities. To them, the doctrinal system of Islam rests on tawhid (monotheism), which means that just as a house has a builder other than itself, so the world has a transcendent Creator other than itself. Also, the basis of man's relationship with the enjoyments of this world is, in their view, zuhd (abstinence). In their definition of zuhd, it means refraining from the ephemeral pleasures of this world in order to attain the ever-lasting enjoyments of the Hereafter. Besides these, there are a series of simple and practical rituals and laws that are handled by fiqh.

Therefore, in this group's view, that which the 'urafa' call tawhid is an idea that goes beyond the simple monotheism of Islam; for the 'arif's view of tawhid is existentialist monism in the sense that he believes that nothing exists except God, His Names, Attributes, and manifestations.

The 'arif's conception of the spiritual path (sayr wa suluk), likewise, they say, also goes beyond the zuhd enjoined by Islam, for the spiritual path of 'irfan involves a number of ideas and concepts - such as love of God, annihilation in God, epiphany - that are not to be found in Islamic piety.

Similarly, the 'arif's concept of the Tariqah goes beyond the Shari'ah of Islam; for the practice of the Tariqah involves matters unknown to fiqh.

Furthermore, in the view of this group, the pious among the Holy Prophet's Companions whom the 'urafa' claim to be their precursors were no more than pious men. Their souls knew nothing of the spiritual path of 'irfan and its tawhid. They were simple otherworldly people who abstained from worldly pleasures and directed their attention to the Hereafter and whose souls were dominated by mixed feelings of fear and hope - fear of the punishment of Hell and hope of the rewards of Paradise. That is all.

In reality this view can in no way be endorsed. The primal sources of Islam are far more extensively richer than what this group - out of ignorance or knowingly - supposes. Neither the Islamic concept of tawhid is as simple and empty as they suppose, nor Islam limits man's spirituality to a dry piety, nor were the pious Companions of the Holy Prophet simple ascetics, nor is the Islamic code of conduct confined to the actions of bodily limbs and organs.

In this lecture, brief evidence will be produced that will suffice to show that Islam's fundamental teachings are capable of having inspired a chain of profound spiritual ideas, both in the theoretical and the practical realms of 'irfan. However, the question of the extent to which the Islamic mystics have used and benefited from Islam's fundamental teachings and the extent to which they may have deviated, is one that we cannot go into in these short lectures.

On the subject of tawhid, the Holy Quran never likens God and the creation to a builder and a house. The Quran identifies God as the Creator of the world, stating at the same time that His Holy Essence is everywhere and with everything:

Wither so ever you turn, there is the Face of God... . (2:115) ... And We are nearer to him than the jugular vein. (50:16) He is the First and the Last, the Outward and the Inward; ... . (57:3) Evidently, these kind of verses represent a call to the thinking minds to a conception of tawhid which goes beyond commonplace monotheism. A tradition of al-Kafi states that God revealed the opening verses of the Sura al-Hadid and the Sura al-'Ikhlas because He knew that in future generations there will emerge people who will think profoundly about tawhid.

As to the spiritual path of 'irfan, in which a series of stages leading to ultimate nearness to God are conceived, it suffices to take into account the Quranic verses which mention such notions as liqa 'Allah (meeting with God), ridwan Allah (God's good pleasure), or those which relate to revelation (wahy), ilham (inspiration), and the angels' speaking to others who are not prophets - for instance, Mary - and especially the verses relating to the Holy Prophet's Ascension (mi'raj; 17:1).

In the Quran there is mention of the 'commanding self' (al-nafs al-'ammarah; 12:53), the 'self-accusative self' (al-nafs al-lawwamah; 75:2), and the 'contented self' (al-nafs al-mutma'innah; 89:27). There is mention of 'acquired knowledge' (al-'ilm al-'ifadi) and inspired knowledge (al-'ilm al-ladunni; 18:65), and of forms of guidance resulting from spiritual struggle:

And those who struggle in Us, We will surely guide them to Our paths ... (29:69) Mention is made in the Quran of the purification of the self, and it is counted as one of the things leading to salvation and deliverance:

(By the self) ... verily he who purifies it has succeeded, while he who corrupts it has indeed failed. (91:7-10) There is also repeated mention there of love of God as a passion above all other human loves and attractions.

The Quran also speaks about all the particles of creation glorifying and praising God (17:44), and this is phrased in a way to imply that if one were to perfect his understanding, he would be able to perceive their praise and magnification of God. Moreover, the Quran raises the issue of the Divine breath in relation to the nature and constitution of the human being (32:9).

This, and much more besides, is sufficient to have inspired a comprehensive and magnificent spirituality regarding God, the world, and man, particularly regarding his relationship with God.

As previously mentioned, we are not considering how the Muslim 'urafa' have made use of these resources, or whether their utilization has been correct or incorrect. We are considering whether there did exist such great resources that could have provided effective inspiration for 'irfan in the Islamic world. Even if we suppose that those usually classed as 'urafa' could not make proper use of them, others who are not classed as such did make use of them.

In addition to the Quran, the traditions, sermons, supplications (du'a'), polemical dialogues (ihtijajat)* and the biographies of the great figures of Islam, all show that the spiritual life current in the early days of Islam was not merely a lifeless type of asceticism blended with a worship performed in the hope of the rewards of Paradise. Concepts and notions are found in the traditions, sermons, supplications, and polemical dialogues that stand at a very high level of sublimity. Similarly, the biographies of the leading personalities of the early days of Islam display many instances of spiritual ecstasy, visions, occurrences, inner insights, and burning spiritual love. We will now relate an example of it.

Al-Kafi relates that one morning after performing the dawn prayer, a young man (Harithah ibn Malik ibn Nu'man al-'Ansari) caught the Prophet's eye. Lean and pale, his eyes sunken, he gave the impression of being unaware of his own condition and of being unable to keep his balance. "How are you?" inquired the Prophet . "I have attained certain faith," the youth replied. "What is the sign of your certainty?" the Prophet asked.

The youth replied that his certainty had immersed him in grief. It kept him awake at night (in worship) and thirsty by day (in fasting), and had separated him from the world and its matters so completely that it seemed to him as if he could see the Divine Throne already set up (on the Judgement Day) to settle the people's accounts, that he together with all of mankind were raised from the dead. He said that it seemed to him that even at that moment he could see the people of Paradise enjoying its bounties, and the people of hell suffering torments and he could hear the roar of its flames.

The Holy Prophet (S) turned to his Companions and told them, "This is a man whose heart has been illuminated with the light of faith by God". Then he said to the youth, "Preserve this condition you are in, and do not let it be taken away from you." "Pray for me," the youth replied, "that God may grant me martyrdom."

Not long after this encounter, a battle took place, and the youth, taking part, was granted his wish and was martyred.

The life, utterances and prayers of the Holy Prophet (S) are rich with spiritual enthusiasm and ecstasy, and full of the indications of gnosis, and the 'urafa' often rely on the Prophet's supplications as reference and evidence for their views.

Similarly, the words of Amir al-Mu'minin 'Ali (A), to whom nearly all the 'urafa' and sufis trace the origin of their orders, are also spiritually inspiring. I wish to draw attention to two passages of the Nahj al-balaghah. In Khutbah No. 222, 'Ali states:

Certainly, God, the glorified, has made His remembrance the means of burnishing the hearts, which makes them hear after deafness, see after blindness, and makes them submissive after unruliness. In all the periods and times when there were no prophets, there have been individuals with whom God - precious are His bounties - spoke in whispers through their conscience and intellects.In Khutbah No. 220, speaking about the men of God, he says:

He revives his intellect and mortifies his self, until his body becomes lean and his coarseness turns into refinement. Then an effulgence of extreme brightness shines forth for illuminating the path before him, opening all the doors and leading him straight to the gate of safety and the (permanent) abode. His feet, carrying his body, become fixed in the position of safety and comfort on account of that which engages his heart and on having won the good pleasure of his Lord.The Islamic supplications, especially those of the Shi'ah, are also replete with spiritual teachings. The Du'a' Kumayl, the Du'a' Abi Hamzah, the supplications of al-Sahifat al-Kamilah and the group of supplications called Sha'baniyyah, all contain the most sublime spiritual ideas.

With the existence of all these resources in Islam, is there a need for us to search for the origin of Islamic 'irfan elsewhere?

This reminds us of the case of Abu Dharr al-Ghifari and his protest against the tyrants of his time and his vocal criticism of their practices. Abu Dharr was severely critical of the favoritism, partisan politics, injustice, corruption and tyranny of the post-Prophetic era in which he lived. This led him to suffer torture and exile, and finally it was in exile, deserted and alone, that he passed away from this world.

A number of orientalists have raised the question of what motivated Abu Dharr to act as he did. They are in search of something foreign to the world of Islam to explain his behavior.

George Jurdaq, a Lebanese Christian, provides an answer to these orientalists in his book al-'Imam 'Ali, sawt al-'adalah al-'insaniyyah (Imam 'Ali, the Voice of Human Justice). There he says that he is amazed at those who wish to trace Abu Dharr's mentality to an extra-Islamic source. He says it is as if they see someone standing at the side of a sea or river with a pitcher of water in his hands, and begin to wonder from which pool he has filled his pitcher, and then, completely ignoring the nearby sea or river, go off in search of a pool or pond to explain his full pitcher of water.

What other source other than Islam could have inspired Abu Dharr? Which source could have the power of Islam in inspiring the likes of Abu Dharr to rise against the tyrants of this world such as Mu'awiyah?

Now we see a similar pattern in regard to 'irfan. The orientalists are in search of a non-Islamic source of inspiration of 'irfan, while they completely overlook the great ocean of Islam.

Can we really be expected to overlook all these resources - the Holy Quran, the traditions, the sermons, the polemical dialogues, the supplications, and the biographies - simply in order to give credence to the view of a group of orientalists and their Eastern followers?

Formerly, the orientalists took great pains to project the origins of Islamic 'irfan as lying outside the original teachings of Islam. Lately, however, such individuals as the English R.A. Nicholson and the French Louis Massignon, after having made extensive studies in Islamic 'irfan, without being unacquainted with Islam in general, have expressly admitted that the principal sources of 'irfan are the Quran and the Prophet's Sunnah.

We will conclude this lecture by quoting a passage by Nicholson from the book The Legacy of Islam:

(Though Muhammad left no system of dogmatic or mystical theology, the Qur'an contains the raw materials of both. Being the outcome of feeling than reflection, the Prophet's statements about God are formally inconsistent, and while Muslim scholastics have embodied in their creed the aspect of transcendence, the Sufis, following his example, have combined the transcendent aspect with that of immanence, on which, though it is less prominent in the Qur'an, they naturally lay greater emphasis.)[2] 'Allah is the Light of the heavens and the earth' (xxiv:35); 'He is the first and the last and the outward and the inward' (lvii:3); 'there is no god but He; everything is perishing except His Face' (xxviii:88); 'Have breathed into him (man) of My spirit' (xv:29); 'Verily, We have created man and We know what his soul suggests to him, for We are nigher unto him than the neck-artery' (1:15); 'wheresoever ye turn, there is the Face of Allah' (ii:114); 'he to whom Allah giveth no light hath no light at all' (xxiv:40). Surely the seeds of mysticism are here. And, for the early Sufis, the Qur'an is not only the Word of God: it is the primary means of drawing near to Him. By fervent prayer, by meditating profoundly on the text as a whole and in particular on the mysterious passages (xvii:1; liii:1-18) concerning the Night journey and Ascension, they endeavored to reproduce the Prophet's mystical experience in themselves.[3] ... The doctrine of a mystical union imparted by divine grace goes beyond anything in the Qur'an, but is stated plainly in apocryphal traditions of the Prophet, e.g. God said, "My servant draws nigh unto Me by works of supererogation, and I love him; and when I love him, I am his ear, so that he hears by Me, and his eye, so that he sees by Me, and his tongue, so that he speaks by Me, and his hand, so that he takes by Me."[4] As repeatedly said before, we are not concerned here with the question whether the 'urafa' have succeeded in correctly utilizing the inspiration provided by Islam; our purpose was to consider whether the main source of their inspiration lay within Islam or outside it.

A Brief History:
The previous lecture dealt with the question of locating the principal origin of Islamic 'irfan, that is, whether there exists in the teachings of Islam and the lives of the Holy Prophet and the Imams a precedent that could have inspired a series of profound and subtle mystical ideas, on a theoretical level, and which could have prompted spiritual enthusiasm and mystical elation on a practical level. The answer to this question was seen to be positive. Now we will continue this discussion.

The genuine teachings of Islam and the lives of its spiritual leaders, so rich with spirituality and spiritual splendor, which have provided the inspiration for profound spirituality in the Islamic world, are not encompassed by that which is termed as 'irfan or sufism. However, it is beyond the scope of these lectures to discuss other parts of Islamic teachings that do not bear this name. We will continue our discussion on the branch that is labeled as 'irfan or sufism, and obviously the limited scope of these lectures does not permit us to go into a critical research. Here we will try to give an outline of the currents and events that have occurred within this branch. For this purpose, it appears to be appropriate that we begin by providing a simple history of 'irfan or Sufism from the beginnings of Islam until at least the 10th/16th century, before turning, so far as is practical in a venture such as this, to an analysis of the issues of 'irfan.

What seems certain is that in the early era of Islam, that is throughout the 1st/7th century at least, there existed no group amongst the Muslims known as 'urafa' or sufis. The name sufi was first used in the 2nd/8th century.

The first person to be called by the name sufi is Abu Hashim al- Kufi. He lived in the 2nd/8th century and he it was who first built at Ramlah, in Palestine, a hospice for worship by a group of ascetically- minded Muslims.[5] The date of Abu Hashim's death is not known, but he was the teacher of Sufyan al-Thawri who died in 161/777.

Abu al-Qasim Qushayri, himself an eminent 'arif and sufi, states that the name sufi had appeared before the year 200/815. Nicholson also states that the name appeared towards the end of the 2nd century H. From a tradition contained in kitab al-ma'ishah (vol. V) of al-Kafi, it appears that a group - Sufyan al-Thawri and a number of others - existed in the time of al-'Imam al-Sadiq (A) (that is to say, during the first half of the 2nd century H.) who were already called by this name.

If Abu Hashim al-Kufi was the first to be called sufi, then, since he was the teacher of Sufyan al-Thawri who died in 161/777, this name was first used during the first half of the 2nd century H., not at its end (as Nicholson and others have stated). Nor does there appear to be any doubt that the reason for the name being sufiyyah was their wearing of wool (sufi: wool). Due to their asceticism, the sufis abstained from wearing fine garments, and instead followed a practice of wearing clothes made of coarse wool.

As for the date this group first began to call themselves 'urafa', again there is no precise information. All that is certain, as confirmed by the remarks quoted of Sari Saqati (d. 243/867)[6], is that the term was current in the third century H. However, in the book al-Luma' of Abu Nasr al-Sarraj al-Tusi, one of the reliable texts of 'irfan and sufism, a phrase is quoted of Sufyan al-Thawri which gives the impression that this term appeared sometime in the second century. [7]

At all events, there was no group known as sufis during the first century H. This name appeared in the 2nd century H., and it seems that it was during the same century that the sufis emerged as a particular group, not in the third century as is the belief of some people. [8]

However, even though no special group existed in the first century by the name of 'urafa' or sufis or any other name, it does not imply that the eminent Companions were merely pious and ascetic persons and that all of them led lives of simple faith devoid of spiritual depth. Perhaps it is true that some of the pious Companions knew nothing more beyond mere piety and worship, yet a group of them possessed a powerful spiritual life. Nor were they all of the same level. Even Salman and Abu Dharr were not of the same degree. Salman enjoyed a degree of faith that Abu Dharr could not have withstood. Many traditions have come to us telling us:

If Abu Dharr knew what was in Salman's heart, he would (considering him a heretic) have killed him. [9] Now we will list the different generations of the 'urafa' and sufis from the 2nd/8th to the 10/16th century.

'Urafa' of the Second/Eighth Century:

1. Al-Hasan al-Basri

The history of what is termed as 'irfan, like kalam, begins with al-Hasan al-Basri (d. 110/728). He was born in 22/642 and lived for eighty-eight years, having spent nine-tenths of his life in the first century H.

Of course, al-Hasan al-Basri was never known by the term sufi, but there are three reasons for counting him amongst the sufis. The first is that he compiled a book called Ri'ayah li huquq Allah (Observance of the Duties to Allah) [10], which can be recognized as the first book on sufism. A unique manuscript of this book exists at Oxford. Nicholson has this to say on the subject:

The first Muslim to give an experimental analysis of the inner life was Harith al-Muhasibi of Basrah ... 'The Path' (tariqah), as described by later writers, consists of acquired virtues (maqamat) and mystical states (ahwal). The first stage is repentance or conversion; then comes a series of others, e.g. renunciation, poverty, patience, trust in God, each being a preparation for the next.[11] Secondly, the 'urafa' themselves trace their orders back to al- Hasan al-Basri; and from him to 'Ali (A), such as the chain of the shaykhs of Abu Sa'id ibn Abi al-Khayr.[12] Similarly, Ibn al-Nadim, in his famous al-Fihrist, traces the chain of Abu Muhammad Ja'far al-Khuldi back to al-Hasan al-Basri, stating that al-Hasan al-Basri had met seventy of the Companions who had fought at Badr.

Thirdly, some of the stories related of al-Hasan al-Basri give the impression that he was in fact part of a group that in later times became known as sufis. We will relate some of these stories when appropriate later on.

2. Malik ibn Dinar:
He was one of those who took asceticism and abstinence from pleasure to the extreme. Many stories are told about him in this regard. He died in the year 130/747.

3. Ibrahim ibn Adham:
The famous story of Ibrahim ibn Adham resembles that of Buddha. It is said that he was the ruler of Balkh when something happened that caused him to repent and enter the ranks of the sufis.
'Urafa' attach great importance to this man, and a very interesting tale is told about him in Rumi's Mathnawi. He died around the year 161/777.

4. Rabi'ah al-'Adawiyyah:
This woman is one of the wonders of her time (d. 135/752 or 185/801). She was named Rabi'ah because she was the fourth daughter of her family (rabi'ah: fem. gender of fourth). She is not to be confused with Rabi'ah al-Shamiyyah, who was also a mystic and a contemporary of Jami and lived in the 9th/15th century.
Lofty sayings and soaring mystical verses are recorded of Rabi'ah al-'Adawiyyah,' and she is noted for amazing spiritual states (halat).

5. Abu Hashim al-Sufi of Kufah:
The date of this man's death is unknown. All that we can say is that he was the teacher of Sufyan al- Thawri; who died in 161/777. He appears to be the first person to have been called sufi. Sufyan says about him: "If it were not for Abu Hashim I would not have known the precise details of ostentation (riya')."

6. Shaqiq al-Balkhi:
He was the pupil of Ibrahim ibn Adham. According to the author of Rayhanat al-'adab, and others quoted in Kashf al-ghummah of 'Ali ibn 'Isa al-'Arbili and Nur al-'absar of al-Shablanji, he once met al-'Imam Musa ibn Ja'far (A) and has given an account of the Imam's great station and miracles. Shaqiq died in 194/810.

7. Ma'ruf al-Karkhi:

He is one of the famous 'urafa'. It is said that his parents were Christian and that he became a Muslim at the hands of al- 'Imam al-Rida (A), learning much from him.

The lines of many orders, according to the claims of the 'urafa', go back to Ma'ruf, and through him to al-'Imam al-Rida, and through al- 'Imam al-Rida to the preceding Imams and thus to the Prophet himself. This chain is therefore termed the 'golden chain' (silsilat al-dhahab). Those known as the Dhahabiyyun generally make this claim.

8. Al-Fudayl ibn 'Iyad:

Originally from Merv, he was an Iranian of Arab descent. It is said of him that at first he was a highwayman, and that as he was preparing to carry out a robbery one night he heard the voice of his potential victim, reciting the Quran. This had such an effect on him that he experienced a change of heart and repented. The book Misbah al-Shariah is attributed to him and it is said to consist of a series of lessons that he took from al-'Imam Ja'far al-Sadiq (A). This book is considered reliable by an erudite scholar of traditions of the last century, the late Hajj Mirza Husayn Nuri, in the epilogue to his Mustadrak al-Wasa'il. Fudayl died in 187/803.

'Urafa' of the Third/Ninth Century:
1. Abu Yazid al-Bistami (Bayazid):

One of the great mystics, it is said Bayazid was the first to speak openly of 'annihilation of the self in God' (fana fi 'Allah') and 'subsistence through God' (baqa' bi 'Allah).

He has said "I came forth from Bayazid-ness as a snake from its skin."

His ecstatic ejaculations (shathiyyat) have led others to call him a heretic. However, the 'urafa' themselves consider him one of those given to mystical 'intoxication' (sukr), that is, he uttered these words when he was beside himself in ecstasy.

Abu Yazid died in 261/874 or 264/877. Some have claimed that he worked as a water carrier in the house of al-'Imam Ja'far al-Sadiq (A). However, this claim is not supported by history; Abu Yazid was not a contemporary of the Imam.

2. Bishr ibn al-Harith al-Hafi:

One of the famous sufis, he was another who led a corrupt life and then repented.

In his book Minhaj al-karamah, al-'Allamah al-Hilli has related an account that depicts Bishr's repentance as being at the hands of al-'Imam

Musa ibn Ja'far (A), and because at the moment of his repentance he was barefoot in the street, he became known as 'al- Hafi' (hafi=barefooted). However, others have given a different reason for his being known as al-Hafi.

Bishr al-Hafi (born near Merv c. 150/767) died in 226/840 or 227/841 in Baghdad.

3. Sari al-Saqati:

One of the friends and companions of Bishr al-Hafi, Sari al-Saqati was one of those who bore affection for the creatures of God and of those who preferred others above themselves.

In his book Wafayat al-'a'yan, Ibn Khallikan writes that Sari once said, "It is thirty years that I have been seeking forgiveness for one phrase, Praise be Allah's, that I allowed to pass my lips." When asked to explain he replied, "One night the bazaar caught fire, and I left my house to see if the fire had reached my shop. When I heard that my shop was safe, I said, 'Praise be Allah's'. Instantly I was brought to my senses with the realization that, granted my shop was unharmed, should I not have been thinking about others'?"

Sa'di is referring to this same story (with slight variations) where he says: One night someone's chimney kindled a fire, And I heard that half of Baghdad had burnt down. One said, thank God that in the smoke and ashes, My shop has not been damaged. A man who had seen the world replied, O selfish man, Was your grief for yourself and no other? Would you be satisfied that a town should burn down by fire, If your own dwelling were left unscathed?

Sari was the pupil and disciple (murid) of Ma'ruf al-Karkhi, and the teacher and maternal uncle of Junayd of Baghdad. Sari has many sayings on mystical unity (tawhid), love of God and other matters. It was also he who said: "Like the sun, the 'arif shines on all the world; like the earth, he bears the good and evil of all; like water, he is the source of life for every heart; and like fire he gives his warmth to all and sundry." Sari died in 253/867 at the age of ninety-eight.

4. Harith al-Muhasibi:

He was one of the friends and companions of Junayd. He was called 'al-muhasibi' due to his great diligence in the matter of self-observation and self-reckoning (muhasabah). He was a contemporary of Ahmad ibn Hanbal, who, being an opponent of 'ilm al-kalam, rejected Harith al-

Muhasibi for entering into theological debates, and this led to the people avoiding him. Born in Basrah in 165/781, he died in 243/857.

5. Junayd of Baghdad:

Originally from Nahaw and, the 'urafa' and sufis have given Junayd the title Sayyid al-Ta'ifah, just as the Shi'ah jurisprudents call al-Shaykh al-Tusi Shaykh al-Ta'ifah.

Junayd is counted as one of the moderate mystics. The kind of ecstatic ejaculations uttered by others were never heard from his lips. He did not even put on the usual dress of the sufis, and dressed like scholars and jurisprudents. It was suggested to him that for the sake of his associates he should wear the sufi dress. He replied: "If I thought clothes were of any impcitance I would make an outfit of molten iron, for the call of truth is that:

There is no significance in the (sufi) cloak, Importance lies only in the (inward) glow.Junayd's mother was the sister of Sari Saqati and Junayd became his pupil and disciple. He was also the pupil of Harith al-Muhasibi. It seems that he died in Baghdad in 298f910 at the age of ninety.

6. Dhu al-Nun al-Misri:

An Egyptian, he was the pupil in jurisprudence of the famous jurisprudent Malik ibn Anas. Jami has called him the leader of the sufis. He it was who first began to use symbolic language and to explain mystical matters through the use of a symbolic terminology which only the elect could understand.

Gradually this became the standard practice, and mystical concepts were expressed in the form of love-poetry (ghazal) and symbolic expressions. Some believe that Dhu al-Nun also introduced many Neoplatonic ideas into 'irfan and sufism.[13] Dhu al-Nun died in 246/860 in Cairo.

7. Sahl ibn 'Abd Allah al-Tustari:

He is one of the great 'urafa' and sufis. A sect of gnostics who consider the main principle of spirituality to be combatting the self is named 'Sahliyyah' after him. He associated with Dhu al-Nun of Egypt at Mecca. He died in Basrah in 282/895. [14]

8. Husayn ibn Mansur al-Hallaj:

Now famous simply as al-Hallaj, he is one of the most controversial mystics of the Islamic world. The shathiyyat uttered by him are many, and he was accused of apostasy and claiming divinity. The jurisprudents

pronounced him an apostate and he was crucified during the reign of the
'Abbasid caliph al-Muqtadir. The 'urafa' themselves accuse him of dis-
closing spiritual secrets. Hafiz has this to say about him:

He said, that friend, who was raised high on the cross, His crime was
that he used to reveal secrets.Some consider him no more than a juggler,
but the 'urafa' themselves absolve him and say that the statements of al-
Hallaj and Bayazid that gave the impression of unbelief were made
when they were beside themselves in the state of 'intoxication'.
Al-Hallaj is remembered by the 'urafa' as a martyr. He was executed in
309/913. [15]

'Urafa' of the Fourth/Tenth Century:
1. Abu Bakr al-Shibli:
A pupil and disciple of Junayd of Baghdad and one who had met al-
Hallaj, al-Shibli is one of the famous mystics. He was originally from
Khurasan. In the book Rawdat al-jannat, and in other biographies, many
mystical poems and sayings have been recorded of him.
 Khawajah 'Abd Allah al-'Ansari has said: "The first person to speak in
symbols was Dhu al-Nun of Egypt. Then came Junayd and he systemat-
ized this science, extended it, and wrote books on it. Al-Shibli, in his
turn, took it to the pulpit." Al-Shibli; died in 334/846 at the age of 87.

2. Abu 'Ali al-Rudbari:
He traced his descent to Nushirwan and the Sasanids, and was a disciple
of Junayd. He studied jurisprudence under Abu al-'Abbas ibn Shurayh,
and literature under Tha'lab. Due to his versatile knowledge, he was
called the 'collector of the Law, the Way, and the Reality' (jami' al-
Shari'ah wa al-Tariqah wa al-Haqiqah). He died in 322/934.

3. Abu Nasr al-Sarraj al-Tusi:
Abu Nasr al-Sarraj is the author of the book al-Luma', one of the principal, ancient and reliable texts of 'irfan and sufism. Many of the shaykhs of
the sufi orders were his direct or indirect pupils. He passed away in 378/
988 in Tus.

4. Abu Fadl ibn al-Hasan al-Sarakhsi:
He was the pupil and disciple of Abu Nasr al-Sarraj, and the teacher of
Abu Sa'id ibn Abi al-Khayr. He was a mystic of great fame. He died in
400/1009.

5. Abu 'Abd Allah al-Rudbari:

He was the son of Abu 'Ali al-Rudbari's sister. He is counted as one of the mystics of Damascus and Syria. He died in 369/979.

6. Abu Talib al-Makki:

The fame of Abu Talib al-Makki rests largely on the book he authored on 'irfan and sufism, Qut al-qulub. This book is one of the principal and earliest texts of 'irfan and sufism. He passed away in 385/995 or 386/996.

'Urafa' of the Fifth/Eleventh Century:

1. Shaykh Abu al-Hasan al-Khurqani:

One of the most famous 'urafa', the 'urafa' relate amazing stories about him. Amongst these is one according to which he would go to the grave of Bayazid and converse with his spirit, taking his advice in solving his difficulties. Rumi says:

After many years had passed since the death of Bayazid Bu'l-Hasan appeared. Now and then he would go and sit By the side of his grave in his presence, Until came the spirit of his shaykh, And as soon as he uttered his problem, it was solvedRumi has remembered Shaykh Abu al-Hasan a lot in his Mathnawi, which shows his devotion and attachment to him. It is said that he met with Abu 'Ali Sina, the philosopher, and with Abu Sa'id ibn Abi al- Khayr, the famous 'arif. He died in 425/1033-34.

2. Abu Sa'id ibn Abi al-Khayr:

One of the most famous of all mystics, Abu Sa'id ibn Abi al-Khayr is also one of those most noted for their spiritual states (halat). When once asked the definition of tasawwuf, he replied: "Tasawwuf is that you give up whatever is on your mind, give away whatever is in your hand, and to give over yourself to whatever you are capable of."

He met with Abu 'Ali Sina. One day Abu 'Ali participated in a meeting at which Abu Sa'id was preaching. Abu Sa'id was speaking about the necessity of deeds, and about obedience and disobedience to God. Abu 'Ali recited these verses (ruba'i):

We are those who have befriended your forgiveness, And seek riddance from obedience and disobedience. Wherever your favour and grace is to be found, Let the not-done be like the done, the done like the not-done. Abu Sa'id immediately replied:

O you who have done no good, and done much bad, And then aspire after your own salvation, Do not rely on forgiveness, for never Was the not-done like the done, the done like the not-done. The following ruba'i is also of Abu Sa'id:

Tomorrow when the six directions fade away, Your worth will be the worth of your awareness. Strive for virtue, for on the Day of Retribution, You shall rise in the form of your qualities. Abu Sa'id passed away in the year 440/1048.

3. Abu 'Ali al-Daqqaq al-Nishaburi:

He is considered one of those who combined in himself the expertise of the Shari'ah and the Tariqah. He was a preacher and an exegete (mufassir) of the Quran. To such an extent did he use to weep while reciting supplications (munajat) that he was given the title 'the lamenting shaykh' (shaykh-e nawhahgar). He passed away in 405/1014 or 412/ 1021.

4. Abu al-Hasan 'Ali ibn 'Uthman al-Hujwiri:

He is the author of Kashf al-Mahjub, one of the famous sufi books and one which has recently been published. He died in 470/1077.

5. Khwajah 'Abd Allah al-'Ansari:

A descendant of the great Companion of the Prophet, Abu Ayyub al-'Ansari, Khwajah 'Abd Allah is himself one of the most famous and pious of all 'urafa'. His fame rests largely on his elegant aphorisms, munajat, and ruba'iyyat.

Amongst his sayings is this:

When a child you are low, when a youth you are intoxicated, when old you are decrepit; so when will you worship God?He has also said:

Returning evil for evil is the trait of a dog; returning good for good is the trait of a donkey; returning good for evil is the work of Khwajah 'Abd Allah al-'Ansari.The following ruba'i is also his:

It is a great fault for a man to remain aloof, Setting oneself above all the creation. Learn thy lesson from the pupil of the eye, That sees everyone but not itself. Khwajah 'Abd Allah was born in Herat where he died and was buried in 481/1088. For this reason he is known as 'the Sage of Herat' (Pir-e Herat).

Khwajah 'Abd Allah authored many books, the best-known of which, Manazil al-sa'irin, is a didactic manual on sayr wa suluk. It is one of the most well-written works of 'irfan, and many commentaries have been written on it.

6. Imam Abu Hamid Muhammad al-Ghazali:

One of the best-known scholars of Islam whose fame has penetrated the East and the West, he combined in his person the knowledge of the rational and traditional sciences (ma'qul wa manqul). He became head of the Nizamiyyah Academy in Baghdad and held the highest position of his age accessible to any scholar. However, feeling that neither his knowledge nor his position could satisfy his soul, he withdrew from public life and engaged in disciplining and purifying his soul.

He spent ten years in Palestine, far from all who knew him, and it was during this period that he became inclined towards 'irfan and sufism. He never again accepted any post or position. Following his period of solitary asceticism, he wrote his famous Ihya' 'ulum al-Din ('Reviving the Sciences of Religion'). He died in his home city of Tus in the year 505/1111.

'Urafa' of the Sixth/Twelfth Century:
1. 'Ayn al-Qudat al-Hamadani:

Of the most enthusiastic of mystics, 'Ayn al-Qudat al-Hamadani was the disciple of Ahmad al-Ghazali's, younger brother of Muhammad, who was also a mystic. The author of many books, he also composed some brilliant poetry that, however, was not altogether free of theopathetic exclamations (shathiyyat). Charges of heresy were brought against him; he was executed, and his body burnt and his ashes cast to the winds. He was killed around 525-533/ 1131-1139.

2. Sanai Ghaznawi:

A famous poet, his verse is loaded with profound mystic sentiments. Rumi, in his Mathnawi, has cited some of his sayings and expounded them. He died around the middle of the 6th/12th century.

3. Ahmad Jami:

Known as "Zhand-e Pil", Jami is one of the most celebrated of 'urafa' and sufis. His tomb lies at Turbat-e Jam, near the border between Iran and Afghanistan, and is well-known. Following lines are among the verses he composed on fear (khawf) and hope (raja'):

Be not haughty, for the mount of many a mighty man Has been hamstrung among rocks in the desert; But neither despair, for even wine-drinking libertines Have suddenly arrived at the destination by a single song. Similarly, on moderation between generosity and thrift he offers the following advice:

Be not like an adze, drawing all to yourself, Nor like a plane, gaining nothing for your work; In matters of livelihood, learn from the saw, It draws some to itself, and lets some scatter. Ahmad Jami died around the year 536/1141.

4. 'Abd al-Qadir al-Gilani:

He is one of the most controversial figures of the Islamic world. To him is attributed the Qadiriyyah order of sufis.

His grave at Baghdad is well known and famous. He is amongst those from whom many supplications and high-flying sayings have been recorded. He was a sayyid descended from al-'Imam al-Hasan (A). He died in 560/1164 or 561/1165.

5. Shaykh Ruzbihan Baqli Shirazi:

He is known as Shaykh-e Shattah on account of his prolific theopathetic exclamations. In recent years some of his books have been published, mainly through the efforts of the orientalists. He died in 606/1209.

'Urafa' of the Seventh/Thirteenth Century:

This century has produced some mystics of the highest stature. We will mention some of them in a chronological order:

1. Shaykh Najm al-Din Kubra:

One of the greatest and most celebrated of mystics, the chains of many orders go back to him. He was the pupil and disciple of Shaykh Ruzbihan, and was also his son-in-law. He had many pupils and disciples, amongst whom was Baha' al-Din Walad, the father of Jalal al-Din Rumi.

He lived in Khuwarizm (in the present day USSR) at the time of the Mongol invasions. Before his city was attacked, he was sent a message informing him that he could lead a party of his family and disciples out of the city to safety. Najm al-Din's reply was that, 'Throughout all the days of comfort I have lived alongside these people. Now that the day of difficulties has come I will not leave them.' He then manfully strapped on a sword and fought alongside the people of the city until he was martyred. This happened in the year 624/1227.

2. Shaykh Farid al-Din al-'Attar:

One of the foremost of mystics, al-'Attar has works both in verse and in prose. His book Tadhkirat al-'awifya' on the lives and characters of the sufis and mystics - which begins with al-'Imam Ja'far al-Sadiq (A) and ends with al-'Imam Muhammad al-Baqir (A) - is considered a source book of documentary significance, and great importance is attached to it by the orientalists.

Similarly, his work Mantiq al-tayr ('The Speech of the Birds') is a master-piece of mystical literature.

Rumi, commenting about al-'Attar and Sana'i, says:

'Attar was the spirit and Sana'i his two eyes, We are following in the steps of Sana'i and 'Attar. Rumi has also said:

'Attar passed through seven cities of love, While we are yet in the bend of a single lane. What Rumi means by the 'seven cities of love' are the seven valleys of which al-'Attar speaks in his Mantiq al-tayr. Muhammad Shabistari in his Gulshan-e raz says:

I am not ashamed of my poetry, For, the like of 'Attar a hundred centuries will not see. Al-'Attar was the pupil and disciple of Shaykh Majd al-Din of Baghdad, who was amongst the pupils and disciples of Shaykh Najm al-Din Kubra. He also benefited from the company of Qutb al-Din Haydar, another of the shaykhs of the age and one after whom the town in which he is buried, Turbat-e Haydariyyah, was named.

Al-'Attar lived during the time of the Mongol invasions, and died - some say at the hands of the Mongols - around 626-28/1228-1230.

3. Shaykh Shihab al-Din al-Suhrawardi:

He is the author of the celebrated 'Awarif al-ma'arif, an excellent text of 'irfan and sufism.

He claimed descent from Abu Bakr. It is said that he went each year to visit Makkah and al-Madinah. He had met and conversed with 'Abd al-Qadir al-Gilani. Amongst his disciples were the famous poets Shaykh Saidi and Kamal al-Din Isma'il al-'Isfahani. Sa'di had this to say about him:

My wise shaykh the murshid, Shihab, gave me two advices: One, not to be egocentric, The other, not to regard others with pessimism. This Suhrawardi is not the same as the famous philosopher known as Shaykh al-'Ishraq, who was killed around 581-590/1185-1194 in Aleppo, Syria. Suhrawardi the gnostic died around the year 632/1234.

4. Ibn al-Farid al-Misri:

He is considered one of the mystics of the first rank. His mystical poetry, in Arabic, reaches the loftiest summits and is of the greatest elegance. His diwan (collection of poems) has been published several times and has been the subject of many distinguished commentaries. Of those who wrote a commentary on his work was 'Abd al-Rahman Jami, a well-known mystic of the ninth century.

The poetry of Ibn al-Farid in Arabic is comparable to that of Hafiz in Persian. Muhyi al-Din ibn al-'Arabi once suggested to him that he should write a commentary on his poems. Ibn al-Farid replied that the commentary of his poems was Ibn al-'Arabi's own al-Futuhat al- Makkiyyah. Ibn al-Farid is of those who went through abnormal 'states' (ahwal). More often than not he was in an ecstatic state and it was in such states that many of his poems were composed. He died in the year 632/1234.

5. Muhyi al-Din ibn al-'Arabi:

One of the descendants of Hatim al-Ta'i, Muhyi al-Din ibn al-'Arabi was originally from Spain. Most of his iife, however, seems to have been spent in Makkah and Syria. He was a pupil of the sixth-century mystic Shaykh Abu Madyan al-Maghribi al-'Andalusi. Through one intermediary link, the chain of his order goes back to the Shaykh 'Abd al-Qadir al-Gilani mentioned above.

Muhyi al-Din, also known by the name Ibn al-'Arabi, is certainly the greatest mystic of Islam. No one else has been able to reach his level, neither before nor after him. Thus he is known by the sobriquet 'al-Shaykh al-'Akbar' (the Greatest Shaykh).

Islamic mysticism, from the time of its first appearance, has made progress one century after another. Each century, as indicated above, produced great mystics who have developed 'irfan, always adding to its heritage. This advancement had always been gradual. But in the 7th/13th century with the appearance of Ibn al-'Arabi 'irfan made a sudden leap and reached the summit of its perfection.

Ibn al-'Arabi took 'irfan to a stage it had never reached before.

The foundations for the second branch of 'irfan, that is theoretical 'irfan and its attendant philosophy, were laid by Ibn al-'Arabi. In general, the mystics who came after him ate the crumbs from his table.

Besides bringing 'irfan into a new phase, Ibn al-'Arabi was one of the wonders of time. He was an amazing person, and this has led to wildly divergent views about him. Some consider him al-Wali al-Kamil (the Perfect Saint) and the Qutb al-'Aqtab (the Pole of Poles). Others degrade him so much as to regard him a heretic, calling him Mumit al-Din (the Killer of the Faith) or Mahi al-Din (the Effacer of the Faith). Sadr al-Muta'allihin (Mulla Sadra), the great philosopher and Islamic genius, had the greatest respect for him, considering him far greater than Ibn Sina or al-Farabi.

Ibn al-'Arabi authored over two hundred books. Many of his works, or perhaps all of those whose manuscripts are extant (numbering about thirty), have been published. Of his most important books, one is his al-Futahat al-Makkiyyah, a colossal work that is a veritable encyclopedia of 'irfan. Another is his Fusus al-hikam which, although brief, is the most precise and most profound text of 'irfan. Numerous commentaries have been written on it, yet perhaps there have been no more than two or three persons in any age who have been able to understand it.

Ibn al-'Arabi passed away in 638/1240 in the city of Damascus, where his grave is still well known even today.

6. Sadr al-Din Qunawi:

He was the pupil, disciple and son of the wife of Ibn al-'Arabi. He was a contemporary of Khwajah Nasir al-Din al-Tusi and of Mawlana Jalal al-Din Rumi. He corresponded with Khwajah Nasir, who paid him great respect. Similarly, at Qunyah(in present day Turkey), there was perfect friendship and cordiality between him and Rumi. Qunawi used to lead the prayers and Rumi would pray behind him, and it has been said that Rumi was his pupil.

There is a story that when one day Rumi came to join Qunawi's circle, he raised himself from his special masnad and offered it to Rumi. Declining, Rumi said that he would have no excuse before God for taking Qunawi's seat. At which Qunawi threw away the masnad, saying, if it did not suit Rumi it would not suit him either.

Qunawi provided the best exposition on the thought and ideas of Ibn al-'Arabi. In fact, without Qunawi it is possible that Ibn al-'Arabi would never have been understood. It was also through Qunawi that Rumi became aquainted with Ibn al-'Arabi and his school, and it seems that the reason for considering Rumi as having been Qunawi's pupil is that Ibn al-'Arabi's ideas are reflected in Rumi's Mathnawi and in his Diwan-e Shams.

Moreover, students of philosophy and 'irfan have used Qunawi's books as textbooks for the last six centuries. His three famous books are: Miftah al-ghayb, al-Nusus and al-FuQuk. Qunawi passed away in 672/1273 (the year in which both Rumi and Khwajah Nasir al-Din died) or in 673/ 1274.

7. Mawlana Jalal al-Din Muhammad Balkhi Rumi:

Known in the East as Mawlawi and in the West as Rumi, author of the world famous Mathnawi, this man is one of the greatest geniuses the world and Islamic 'irfan have ever seen. He was descended from Abu Bakr. His Mathnawi is an ocean of wisdom and full of precise spiritual, social and mystic insights. He ranks amongst the foremost Persian poets. Originally from Balkh, he left it with his father when still a child. Together they visited Makkah, and at Nishabur they met with Shaykh Farid al-Din al-'Attar. On leaving Makkah his father went to Qunyah and there they settled down. At first Rumi, being a scholar, engaged himself, like the other scholars of his rank, in teaching, and he lived a respectable life. Then he met the famous mystic Shams-e Tabrizi. Rumi was magnetized by this man and at once gave everything up. His diwan of ghazal is named after Shams, and he has repeatedly made ardent mention of him in his Mathnawi. Rumi passed away in 672/1273.

8. Fakhr al-Din al-'Iraqi al-Hamadani:
A well-known poet of ghazal and a mystic, he was a pupil of Sadr al-Din Qunawi and a murid and protege of Shihab al-Din al-Suhrawardi. He passed-away in 688/1289.

'Urafa' of the Eighth/Fourteenth Century:
1. 'Ala' al-Dawlah Simnani:
He began as a secretarial official; then he gave up his post to enter the path of the 'urafa', giving up all his wealth in the way of God. He wrote many books, and held special beliefs in the field of theoretical 'irfan, which are discussed in several important texts of 'irfan. He passed away in 736/1335. Amongst his disciples was the well-known poet Khwajawi Kirmani, who describes him thus:
Whoever flourishes upon the path of 'Ali, Like Khidr, finds the springs of life. Getting relief from the whisperings of the Devil, He becomes like 'Ala ' al-Dawlah Simnani.

2. 'Abd al-Razzaq Kashani:
Of the scholars of the eighth century 'irfan, 'Abd al-Razzaq Kashani wrote commentaries on the Fusus of Ibn al- 'Arabi and the Manazil al-sa'irin of Khwajah 'Abd Allah. Both of these have been published and are referred to by scholars.
According to the author of Rawdat al-Jannat, in his account of Shaykh 'Abd al-Razzaq Lahiji, 'Abd al-Razzaq Kashani was eulogized by al-Shahid al-Thani. He and 'Ala' al-Dawlah Simnani had heated discussions on theoretical issues of 'irfan that had been raised by Ibn al- 'Arabi. He passed away in the year 735/1334.

3. Khwajah Hafiz Shirazi:

Despite his world-wide fame, the details of Hafiz's life are not altogether clear. What is known is that he was a scholar, an 'arif, a hafiz of the Quran and an exegete of the Book. He himself has repeatedly indicated this in his verses:

I haven 't seen more beautiful lines than yours, Hafiz, By the Quran that you have in your breast. Your love shall cry out if you, like Hafiz, Recite the Quran memoriter with all the fourteen readings. Of the memorizers of the world none like me has gathered, Subtleties of wisdom with Quranic delicacies. In his poetry Hafiz speaks much of the pir-e tariqat (spiritual guide) and of the murshid (master), yet it is not clear who was the teacher and guide of Hafiz himself.

Hafiz's poetry attains to lofty mystical heights, and there are few people who are able to perceive his mystic subtleties. All the 'urafa' who came after him admit that he had indeed practically covered the lofty stages of 'irfan. Several important scholars have written commentaries on some of his verses. For example, a treatise was written by the well-known philosopher of the ninth century, Muhaqqiq Jalal al-Din Dawwani, on the following verse:

My teachersaid: the pen of creation was subject to no error, Bravo the pure eyes that hide all defects. Hafiz passed away in 791/1389.[17]

4. Shaykh Mahmud Shabistari:

He is the creator of the sublime mystic poem Gulshan-e raz (The Garden of Secrets). This poem is counted as one of the loftiest works of 'irfan, and has immortalized the name of its author. Many commentaries have been written upon it, perhaps the best of which is that written by Shaykh Muhammad Lahiji, which has been published and is available. Shabistari passed away about the year 720/1320.

5. Sayyid Haydar Amuli:

One of the erudite mystics, Sayyid Haydar Amuli is the author of the book Jami' al-'asrar (Collector of the Secrets), which is a precise work on the theoretical 'irfan of Ibn al-'Arabi. This book has lately been published. Another book by him is Nass al-nusus, which is a commentary on Ibn al-'Arabi's Fusus al-hikam.

He was a contemporary of the famous jurisprudent Fakhr al-Muhaqqiqin al-Hilli, but the date of his death is not known.

6. 'Abd al-Karim Jilani:

He is the author of the well-known book al-'Insan al-kamil ('The Perfect Man'). The concept of the perfect man is a subject first raised in its theoretical form by Ibn al-'Arabi, and has ever since occupied an important place in Islamic 'irfan. Ibn al-'Arabi's pupil and disciple, Sadr al-Din Qunawi, has discussed it fully in his Miftah al-ghayb and, as far as we know, at least two mystics have written whole books on the subject. One is 'Aziz al-Din Nasafi, a mystic of the latter half of the 7th/13th century, the other being 'Abd al-Karim Jilani. Jilani passed away in 805/1402 at the age of thirty- eight.

'Urafa' of the Ninth/Fifteenth Century
1. Shah Ni'mat Allah Wali:

He claimed descent from the house of 'Ali. He is amongst the most famous of 'urafa' and sufis. The current Ni'mat- ullahi order is one of the most famous of sufi orders. His grave near the city of Kirman is still a sufi shrine.

It is said that he lived until the age of ninety-five, and died in the year 820/1417, 827/1424 or 834/1430. He lived most of his life in the seventh century and associated with Hafiz Shirazi. Much of his mystical poetry has survived.

2. Sa'in al-Din 'Ali Tarakeh Isfahani:

He is one of the most erudite of 'urafa'. He was deeply acquainted with the theoretical 'irfan of Ibn al-'Arabi. His book Tamhid al-qawa'id, which has been published and is available, is a tribute to his profound learning in 'irfan, and has been used as a source by the scholars who have succeeded him.

3. Muhammad ibn Mamzah al-Fanari al-Rumi:

One of the scholars of the 'Uthmani empire, he distinguished himself in several fields. Author of many books, his fame in 'irfan is due to his book Misbah al-'uns. This is a commentary on Qunawi's Miftah al-ghayb. Although it is not every- one who can write a commentary and exposition on the books of Ibn al-'Arabi and his disciple Sadr al-Din Qunawi, the authorities in 'irfan to have followed him have all confirmed the value of this work. A lithograph print of this book with the hawashi of Aqa Mirza Hashim Rashti, a mystic of the last century, has been published from

Tehran.
Unfortunately due to bad print parts of the hawashi are unreadable.

4. Shams al-Din Muhammad Lahiji Nurbakhshi:

The author of a commentary on the Gulshan-e raz of Mahmud Sh-abistari, and a contemporary of Mir Sadr al-Din Dashtaki and 'Allamah Dawwani, he lived in Shiraz. These two, who were both outstanding philosophers of their age and, according to what Qadi Nur Allah Shushtari has written in his Majalis al-mu'minin, both accorded Lahiji the greatest respect.

Lahiji was the disciple of Sayyid Muhammad Nurbakhsh, himself the pupil of Ibn Fahd al-Hilli. In his commentary on the Gulshan-e raz he traces his chain back from Sayyid Muhammad Nurbakhsh to Ma'ruf al-Karkhi, thence to al-'Imam al-Rida and the preceding Imams and thus to the Holy Prophet himself (S). This he calls the 'Golden Chain' (silsilat al-dhahab).

His fame rests largely on his commentary on the Gulshan-e raz, a commentary that itself is one of the loftiest of mystic texts. He began his writings, according to what he himself relates in the introduction to his commentary, in the year 877/1472. The year of his death is not precisely known. It seems to have been before 900/1494.

5. Nur al-Din 'Abd al-Rahman Jami:

Jami claimed descent from the well- known jurisprudent of the second century, Muhammad ibn al-Hasan al-Shaybani. A powerful poet, he is considered the last great mystic poet of the Persian language.

 At first he assumed the takhallus "Dashti", but since he was born in the locality of Jam, in the vicinity of Mashhad, and traced his spiritual descent to Ahmad Jami (Zhand-e Pil), he changed this to Jami. In his own words:

My birthplace is Jam and the drops of my pen Are the draught of the cup of Shaykh al-Islam,[18] Thus in the pages of my poetry In two ways my pen-name is Jami. Jami was an accomplished scholar in the various fields of Arabic grammar and syntax, law, jurisprudence, logic, philosophy and 'irfan. His many books include a commentary on the Fusus al-hikam of Ibn al- 'Arabi, a commentary on the Luma'at of Fakhr al-Din 'Iraqi, a commentary on the Ta'iyyah of Ibn al-Farid, a commentary on the Qasidat al-Burdah in praise of the Holy Prophet (S), a commentary on the Qasidah Mimiyyah of Farazdaq in praise of al-'Imam 'Ali ibn al-Husayn, a book entitled al-Lawdyih, his Bahdristan, written in the style of Sa'di's Gulistans and a book Nafahat al-'uns on the biographies of mystics.

Jami was the disciple of Baha' al-Din Naqshaband, the founder of the Naqshabandi order. However, as in the instance of Muhammad Lahiji, who was a disciple of Sayyid Muhammad Nurbakhsh, his academic standing is above that of his peer. Jami, even though he is counted as one of the followers of Baha' al-Din Naqshaband, achieved an academic standing several degrees higher than that of Baha' al-Din.

Thus in this brief history in which we are concentrating upon the academic side of 'irfan and not upon the development of the various orders, special mention has been made of Muhammad Lahiji and 'Abd al-Rahman Jami, rather than of the founders of their orders. Jami died in 898/1492 at the age of 81.

This ends our brief history of 'irfan, covering the period from its beginnings until the close of the 9th/15th century. We chose to end at this point because, in our view, from the 10th/16th century onwards 'irfan took on a different form. Up until this time the learned and academic figures of 'irfan had all been members of regular sufi orders and the poles (aqtab) or masters of the sufi orders were great academic figures of 'irfan, to whom we owe the great mystic works. Around the beginning of the 10th/16th century, however, this began to change.

Firstly, the masters of the sufi orders were no longer possessed of the academic prominence of their forerunners. It may be said that from this time onwards formal sufism lost itself in customs, outward aspects, occasionally of an innovative nature (bid'ah).

Secondly, scholars who were not members of any formal sufi order began to show profound learning in the theoretical 'irfan of Ibn al-'Arabi, such that none from amongst the sufi orders could match them. Examples of such scholars are Sadr al-Muta'allihin of Shiraz (d. 1050/1640), his pupil Fayd Kashani (d. 1091/1680), and Fayd's own pupil Qadi Sa'id Qummi (d. 1103/1691). The knowledge of each of these of the theoretical 'irfan of Ibn al-'Arabi exceeded that of the poles or masters of any sufi order of their times, while they themselves were not attached to any of the sufi orders. Moreover, this is a development that has continued down to the present day, as can be seen in the examples of the late Aqa-Muhammad Rida Qumsheh'i and the late Aqa Mirza Hashim Rashti. These two scholars of the last hundred years were both experts in the field of theoretical 'irfan, yet they too were not members of any sufi order.

On the whole, it can be said that it was from the time of Muhyi al-Din

End of Brief history → (handwritten margin note)

ibn al-'Arabi, who laid the foundations of theoretical 'irfan and philosophized 'irfan, that the seed of this new development was sown.

The above-mentioned Muhammad ibn Hamzah Fanari perhaps represented this type. But the new development that produced experts in the field of theoretical 'irfan who were either not at all devoted to practical 'irfan and its spiritual methodology, or, if they were - and to some extent most of them were - had nothing to do with any formal sufi order, is perfectly discernible from the 10th/16th century onwards.

Thirdly, since the 10th/16th century there have been individuals and groups devoted to the spiritual methodology of practical 'irfan, who had attained a very lofty spiritual standing indeed and yet they were not members of any of the formal sufi orders. They were either indifferent to the formal sufis or regarded them as being partially or totally heretical.

Amongst the characteristics of this new group of theoretical and practical 'urafa' - who were also learned in law and jurisprudence - was a perfect loyalty to the shari'ah and a harmony between the rites of the path of progression and the rites of jurisprudence. This development has also its own history, but here we have no opportunity to enter its details.

The Mystic's Stations (Maqamat):

The 'urafa' maintain that in order to arrive at the stage of true gnosis, there are stages and stations that must be covered. Unless covered, the 'urafa' hold, to arrive at the station of true gnosis is impossible.

'Irfan has a facet that it shares with theosophy (hikmat ilahi), while many of the facets of these two disciplines differ. The facet common to them both is that the aim of both is knowledge of God (ma'rifat Allah). They differ in that theosophy does not aim solely at knowledge of God but rather aims at a knowledge of the order of being.

The knowledge that is sought by the theosophist (hakim) is of the system of existence, of which, naturally, knowledge of God is an important pillar. The goal of 'irfan, on the other hand, is exclusively knowledge of God.

In the view of 'irfan, knowledge of God is total knowledge. Everything must be known in the light of knowledge of God and from the point of view of tawhid; such knowledge is a derivative of knowledge of God.

Secondly, the knowledge sought by the hakim is intellectual knowledge and can be likened to the knowledge acquired by the mathematician after thought and reflection on a particular mathematical problem. However, the knowledge sought by the 'arif is experienced and witnessed; it can be likened to the knowledge acquired by an experimental scientist in his laboratory. The hakim seeks certain knowledge ('ilm al-

حکیم
vs
عارف

علم الیقین

43

حکیم ← عقلی
عارف ← قلبی

عین الیقین

yaqin), while the 'arif seeks the certainty of direct vision ('ayn al-yaqin).
Thirdly, the means employed by the hakim are his reason, deductions
and proofs, whereas those employed by the 'arif are the heart and the
purification, disciplining and perfecting of the self. The hakim seeks,
through the telescope of his mind, to study the order of existence, while
the 'arif seeks to prepare the whole of his being so as to arrive at the core
of reality. He seeks to reach reality like a drop of water in the search of
the sea. In the view of the hakim, the perfection expected of a human being lies in understanding reality, while in the 'arif's view it lies in reaching reality. In the hakim's view an imperfect human being is one who is
ignorant, while in the 'arif's view the imperfect human is one who has remained distant and separated from his origin.

The 'arif therefore sees perfection in reaching rather than in understanding. And in order to reach the principal goal and the stage of true gnosis,
he views the traversing of several stages and stations as being necessary
and essential. This he calls sayr wa suluk, the science of inward wayfar-
ing.

These stages and stations have been discussed in great detail in the
books of 'irfan. Here it is not possible to explain, even briefly, each and
every one of them. However, in order at least to give a general impression, I believe that we can do no better than to turn to the ninth section of
Ibn Sina's al-'Isharat. Although Ibn Sina is mainly a philosopher, not a
mystic, he is not a 'dry' philosopher, and especially towards the end of
his life he developed mystic inclinations. In his al-'Isharat, which appears
to be his last work, he has devoted a whole section to the 'stations' of the
gnostics. This section being extraordinarily sublime and beautiful, we
consider it more suitable for our purposes to present a summary of this
section, rather than citing or translating suitable passages from the books
of the 'urafa'.

Zahid, 'abid & 'arif:
He who abstains from the enjoyments of the world, even its wholesome
ones, is called a zahid (ascetic); and he who is careful to perform worship, prayer and fasting and the like, is called an 'abid (devotee); and he
who keeps his thought turned perpetually towards the realm of light in
order that the light of the Real shine in his breast is called an 'arif; and
sometimes two or more of these epithets may apply to the same person.
Although Ibn Sina defines here the zahid, the 'abid and the 'arif, yet at
the same time he is defining zuhd, 'ibadah, and 'irfan. This is because a
definition of zahid, 'abid, or tarif per se includes implicitly a definition of

44

zuhd, 'ibadah, or 'irfan. Thus the conclusion to be drawn from this passage is that zuhd is abstinence from worldly enjoyments; 'ibadah is the performance of specific acts like prayer, fasting, reciting the Quran and the like; and 'irfan is turning away the mind from everything but Allah and paying complete attention to the Divine Essence so that the light of the Real may shine on one's heart.

The last clause indicates an important point. One or more of these characteristics may occur in combination. Thus it is possible for an individual to be an 'abid and a zahid, a zahid and an 'arif, an 'abid and an 'arif, or an 'abid, zahid, and 'arif at one and the same time. Ibn Sina has not elaborated this, but he implies that although it is possible for one to be a zahid or an 'abid and not be an 'arif, it is not possible for one to be an 'arif and not be a zahid and an 'abid. One may be both a zahid and an 'abid without being an 'arif, but an 'arif by definition is also a zahid and an 'abid. So, although not every zahid or 'abid is an 'arif, every 'arif is a zahid and an 'abid.

In the next passage we will see that the zuhd of an 'arif differs in its goal from that of a non-'arif. In fact, the spirit and essence of the 'arif's zuhd and 'ibadah are different from those of the non-'arif:

The zuhd for the non-'arif, is a transaction by which he gives up the pleasures of the world for the pleasures of the Hereafter, whereas for the 'arif it is something through which he dissociates himself from everything that keeps him from attention towards God and he looks down on everything except God. Whereas worship for the non-'arif is a transaction by which he performs actions in the world for a reward (ajr, thawab) to be received in the Hereafter, for the 'arif it is a kind of exercise that is aimed at strengthening his self's intellectual and imaginative faculties, and which, by repetition, draws away the self from the realm of illusion to the realm of the Real.

The 'arif's Goal:

The 'arif desires the Real (God) not for the sake of something else, and he values nothing above his knowledge of the Real, and his worship of Him is because He is worthy of worship and it is a worthy way of relating himself to Him; it is not out of desire (for rewards) or fear (of chastisement).

The meaning of this is that in terms of his aims the 'arif is a muwahhid. He seeks only God, yet his desire of God is not on account of His gifts in this world or in the Hereafter. Were such to be the case, the real object of his desire would be the gifts, God being only the preliminary means by which the desired gifts are sought. In such a case, in reality, the final object of worship and desire would be one's own self; for the purpose of seeking those gifts is the pleasure of the self.

However, the 'arif desires whatever he desires for the sake of God. When he desires the gifts of God he does so because they are from Him, and are His favours. They represent His Grace and Magnanimity. So, while the non-'arif seeks God for the sake of His gifts, the 'arif seeks the gifts of God for the sake of God.

Here the question may arise, if the 'arif does not seek God for the sake of anything, then why does he worship Him? Is it not true that every act of worship must have a purpose? Ibn Sina's passage contains the answer. He states that the goal and motivation of the 'arif's worship is one of two things. One is the inherent worthiness of the Worshipped to be worshipped, meaning that one worships God simply because He is worthy of worship. It is rather like someone who upon noticing some admirable qualities in a person or a thing praises that person or thing. If asked what motivated him to utter such praise, or of what benefit was it to him, he will reply that he sought no benefit from his praise, but simply saw that person or thing as being genuinely deserving of praise. This is true of the praise accorded to the heroes or the champions of each and every field.

The other motivation of the 'arif's worship is the worthiness of worship itself. It bears an intrinsic nobility and beauty of its own, for it is a connection, a tie, between oneself and God. Thus it has a worthiness of its own, and there is no reason why worship should necessarily entail desire or fear.

'Ali (A) has some famous words on this subject:

ما عبدتك
خوفاً
من نارك

My God, I do not worship You in fear of Your Fire, nor in desire for Your Paradise, but I find You worthy of worship so I worship You. The 'urafa' place great importance on this issue, considering it a kind of shirk (polytheism) for one's goal in life and particularly in worship to be something other than God Himself. 'Irfan totally rejects this kind of shirk. Many have written elegantly and subtly on the subject, and we will look at an allegory from Sa'di's Bustan which takes the outward form of a story of Sultan Mahmud of Ghaznah and his close confidant Iyaz:

One with the Shah of Ghaznah found fault, saying, What charm has he, the Shah's friend Iyaz. A flower indeed with neither colour nor smell, How strange of the nightingale to set its heart upon such a thing. Someone conveyed this remark to Sultan Mahmud, Who, on hearing it, was besides himself with anguish. 'I love him for his disposition and character, Nor for his pleasing gait and stature. ' Heard I once that in a narrow defile, The king's treasure-chest broke open after a camel fell. The king, after signalling his bequest, Spurred on his steed to get ahead hastily. The riders now fell upon the pearls and corals, Their thoughts now turning from the king to the treasure. None of the proud lads remained that day To follow in the king's train except Iyaz Looking out, the king saw him, and beholding Iyaz, His face like a flower bloomed with delight. 'What booty have you brought along, ' the king inquired. 'None, 'said, Iyaz. 'I hurried after you, Preferring your service to treasure and bounties.Sa'di then turns from this story to the point he wishes to make, which he expresses thus:

If you look to your friend for his favours, You are tied to yourself not to your friend A breach of the Way it was if the saints Desired of God aught other than God.The First Station

The first level of the 'arif's journey is what they eall 'resolution' (al-'iradah), and this is a fervent desire to catch hold of the Firm Tie (al-'urwat al-wuthqa) that catches hold of one who is perceptive of true proofs, or who has settled his self through the covenant of faith, so that it impels his heart towards the Holy in order to attain the spirit of connection (with Him).

In order to explain the first stage of the spiritual path - which in one respect potentially embraces the whole of 'irfan - we are obliged to be somewhat elaborate. The 'urafa' primarily believe in a principle which they sum up in the following phrase:

The ends are the return to the beginnings.Clearly, for the end to be the beginning there are two possibilities.

One is that the movement is in a straight line, and that once the object in motion reaches a certain point it changes its direction and retraces exactly the same route that it came. In philosophy it has been proved that such a change of direction would entail an interval of motionlessness, even if imperceptible. Furthermore, these two movements would be opposite to each other. The second possibility is that the movement is on along a curve all of whose points are equidistant from a certain central point, in other words a circle. It is clear that if the movement takes the form of a circle, naturally the path will end at the point of commencement.

An object moving in a circle will continually move farther from the point of beginning until it reaches the point farthest from where it began. This is the point diametrically opposite to the point of commencement. It is also from this point that, with no pause or interval, the return journey (ma'ad) to the point of departure (mabda') commences. The 'urafa' call the first part of the journey, i.e. from the point of departure to the point farthest from it, 'the arc of descent' (qaws al-nazul), and the journey from there back to the point of departure, 'the arc of ascent' (qaws al-su'ud). There is a philosophical view associated with the movement of things from the point of departure to the farthest point which the philosophers call the 'principle of causality' (asl al-'illiyyah), and which the 'urafa' call the 'principle of emanation' (asl al-tajalli); in either case objects travelling along the arc of descent are as if driven from behind. Similarly, the movement of objects from the farthest point to the point of departure also has its own philosophical theory. This is the principle of every derivative being's desire and passion to return to its origin. In other words, it is the principle of the flight back of everything estranged and stranded to its origin and homeland. This tendency, so the 'urafa' believe, is inherent in each and every particle of existence, including the human being, though in man it can often be latent and hidden.

Man's preoccupations prevent the activity of this tendency, and a series of stimuli are required before this inner inclination will surface. It is the appearance and surfacing of this inclination that the 'urafa' term as 'resolution' or 'will' (iradah).

Thus in reality this resolution is a type of awakening of a dormant consciousness. 'Abd al-Razzaq Kashani, in his Istilahat, defines iradah as:

A spark in the heart from the fire of love that compels one to answer the summons of the Real (Haqiqah). Khwajah 'Abd Allah Ansari in his Manazil al-sa'irin defines iradah as follows:

It is the voluntary answer (in actions) to the summons of the Real (Haqiqah). Here it is necessary to point out that the meaning of iradah being the first stage is that it is the first stage after a chain of other stages has been passed, stages that are called 'preparations' (bidayat), 'doors' (abwab), 'conduct' (mu'amalat). and 'manners' (akhlaq). Thus iradah is the first stage in the terminology of the 'urafa' in the sense that it signifies a genuine gnostic awakening.

Rumi describes the principle that 'the end is the return to the beginning' as follows:

The parts are faced towards the Whole, Nightingales are in love with the rose's face; Whatever comes from the sea to the sea returns, And everything goes back to its source; Like the streams rushing down from mountain tops, My soul, burning with love, longs to leave the body.Rumi opens his Mathnawi by inviting the reader to listen to the plaintive cries of the reed, as it complains of its separation from the reed bed. Thus in the first lines of his Mathnawi Rumi is actually bringing up the first stage of the 'arif, that is iradah, a desire to return to one's origins that is accompanied with the feeling of separation and loneliness. Rumi says:

Listen to the reed as its story it relates And of its separation it complains. Since the time that from the reed bed was I taken, At my strains have lamented man and woman. O, a heart I seek that is torn with the pain of separation That it may hear the tale of my longing for return. Whoever remains distant from his origins, Seeks again the life of reunion.To sum up, Ibn Sina, in the above passage, means that iradah is a desire and longing that, after deep feelings of alienation, loneliness and estrangement, makes its appearance in the human being and motivates him to seek reunion with the Real, a union which puts an end to the feelings of alienation, loneliness, and helplessness.

Exercise and Self-Discipline:

Then what is certainly required is exercise (riyadah), and it is directed towards three ends - the first is to clear the path of all but the Real; the second is to subjugate the 'commanding self' (al-nafs al-'ammarah) to the 'contented self' (al-nafs al-mutma'innah); the third is to render the heart subtle for awareness.

After having commenced the journey at the stage of iradah, the next stage is that of exercise and preparedness. This preparedness is termed riyadah. Nowadays this term is generally misunderstood and it is taken to mean self-mortification. In some religions the principle of mortifying the self is hallowed. Perhaps the best examples of this are to be seen in the Yogis of India. In the terminology of Ibn Sina, however, the word is not used in this sense. The original meaning of this Arabic word is 'to exercise', or 'to break in a colt.' Thereafter the word was used for physical exercise, a sense which the word still bears today. The 'urafa' borrowed this word, and in their terminology it is used to mean exercising the soul and preparing it for the illumination of the light of knowledge (ma'rifah). It is in this sense that the word is used in the passage above.

Ibn Sina then declares this exercising and preparing of the soul to be directed towards three aims. The first of these is related to external matters and entails the removal of distractive occupations and the causes of negligence (ghaflah). The second is related to the balance of the inner forces and the removal of agitations from the soul, which he has described as the submission of the 'commanding self' to the 'contented self'. The third relates to qualitative changes in the soul, which he calls 'rending subtle of the heart'.

And the first [of the three aims of riyadah] is aided by true zuhd (i.e. zuhd removes the impediments and the hindering preoccupations, which cause neglect, from the path). The second is aided by several things: worship infused with (presence of heart, concentration and) reflection; melody that serves to strengthen the self through which the accompanying words have an effect on the heart (such as melodious reciting of the Quran, supplications and litanies, and the singing of mystic poetry); the instructive speech of a pure, eloquent speaker who speaks gently and effectively in the manner of a guide. As for the third goal, it is aided by subtle thoughts (contemplating subtle and delicate ideas and meanings which lead to spiritual refinement) and a chaste love (a love that is spiritual and not physical and sensual) which is directed by the virtues of the beloved and not ruled over by sensuality.

Then, when iradah and riyadah reach a certain degree, flashes (khalasat) of the dawning light of the Real will descend upon him, delightful as they are, they are momentary like flashes of lightning appearing and instantly vanishing. These they call 'moments' (awqat), and these flashes increase in frequency with greater diligence in riyadah.

As he advances deeper into this, they descend upon him even when he is not exercising. Now often he will glance at something and his glance be deflected from it towards the Holy, bringing to his attention some aspect of the Divine, and a state of trance (ghashyah) descends upon him, in which, as if, he sees God in every thing.

Perhaps it is at this stage that his states overwhelm him, disturbing his equanimity, a change that would be noticed by anyone near him.

Then, he reaches a point in his exercises when his 'moments' change into stable tranquillity, the brief snatches become familiar and the flashes beeome a prolonged blaze. Then he achieves an enduring gnostic state which permanently accompanies him from which he derives an ecstatic delight. And when it departs him he becomes sad and bewildered.

And perhaps it is at this stage the state in which he is in will make itself apparent (to others); but as he progresses deeper into this gnosis, its appearance will be less detectable in him and he will be absent when (appearing to be) present, and travelling when (appearing to be) still.

This passage calls to mind a sentence spoken by 'Ali ibn Abi Talib (A) to his disciple Kumayl ibn Ziyad about the 'friends of God' (awliya' al-Haqq), who exist in every age:

Knowledge has led them to the reality of insight, and they are in contact with the spirit of certainty. They find easy what is regarded as rough by those who live in comfort and luxury. They are intimate with what

terrifies the ignorant. They are in the company of people with their bodies, yet their souls are lodged in the highest realm. (Nahj al-balaghah,
Hikam, No. 147). Until this stage, perhaps, this state of gnosis will occur
to him only occasionally. Thereafter it will gradually become such that it
is available to him whenever he wants.

Thereafter, he advances further than even this stage until his affair no
longer depends on his own wish. Whenever he observes a thing he sees
other than it (i.e God), even if his observation is not for the sake of reflection. So, the opportunity presents itself to ascend from the plane of false
appearances to the plane of Truth. He becomes stabilized upon it, while
(in the world) he is surrounded by the heedless.

Up until this point we have been dealing with the stage of exercise, self-
discipline, struggle and the spiritual itinerary. Now the 'arif has reached
his goal.

When he crosses from the stage of riyadah to that of attainment, his inward becomes like a clear mirror facing in the direction of the Real.
Sublime delights shower upon him, and he rejoices at his self for what is
there of the Real. Now (like one viewing an image in a mirror, who looks
either at the image or at the mirror reflecting the image) he is perplexed
by two views: the view of the Real and the view of his own self.

Then, he becomes oblivious to his own self and views only the Holy.
And if he notices his self it is for the reason of its being the viewer, not
for the sake of its own beauty (like one who when looking at an image in
a mirror, views the image only; although he does not pay attention to the
mirror itself, nevertheless the mirror is seen while viewing the image,
though the mirror is not viewed for its own beauty). It is at this point
that the wayfarer attains union (and his journey from khalq to Haqq becomes complete).

Here ends our summary of the ninth section of Ibn Sina's Isharat and his
account of the journey from creation (khalq) to God (Haqq). A point that
must be added is that the 'urafa' believe in four journeys: sayr min al-
khalq ila al-Haqq, sayr bi al-Haqq a al-Haqq, sayr min al-Haqq ila al-
khalq bi al-Haqq, sayr fi al-khalq bi al-Haqq (the journey from creation
to God; the journey with God in God; the journey with God from God to
creation; and finally, the journey in creation with God).

The first journey is from creatures to the Creator. The second is in the
Creator; it means that in the course of it the 'arif becomes acquainted
with His Qualities and Names and himself becomes adorned with the
same. In the third journey, he returns towards the creation, without becoming separated from God, in order to guide the people. The fourth

journey is amongst the people while still united with God. In this journey the 'arif is with and amongst the people and seeks to guide their affairs so as to lead them towards God.

The summary from Ibn Sina's al-'Isharat given above is related to the first of these journeys. He also gives a brief account of the second journey, but it is not necessary for our purposes to include it. Khwajah Nasir al-Din al-Tusi, in his commentary on al-'Isharat, says that Ibn Sina has explained the first journey of the 'arif in nine stages. Three stages are related to the beginning of the journey, three to the journey from its beginning to its end, and three are related to the arrival or the union. Some reflection on Ibn Sina's account makes the point clear.

By 'riyadah ' which is translated as 'exercise', Ibn Sina means the exercises in self-discipline that the 'arif undergoes. There are many of these, and the 'arif must follow a chain of stations in these exercises too. Here Ibn Sina is brief in the extreme, yet the 'urafa' have discussed this matter in detail, and one may seek these details in their works.

Some Terms of 'Irfan:

In this section we intend to cover some of the special terms used in 'irfan. The 'urafa' have coined a large number of these terms, and without an acquaintance with them it is not possible to understand many of their ideas. In fact, one may draw a conclusion quite opposite to that intended. This is one of the characteristics of 'irfan. However, every branch of learning has its own set of terms, and this is a matter of necessity. The commonly understood meanings of words used are often unable to meet the precise requirements of a science or discipline.

Thus there is no option but that in every discipline certain words be selected to convey certain specific meanings, thus coining for the practitioners of that discipline a special vocabulary. 'Irfan, too, is no exception to this general rule.

Moreover, the 'urafa' insist that none but those initiated to the Path should know their ideas, because - in their view at least - none but the 'urafa' are able to understand these concepts. Thus the 'urafa' unlike the masters of other sciences and crafts, intentionally attempt to keep their meanings concealed so that the vocabulary they devised bears, in addition to the usual aspects of a terminology, also something of an enigmatic aspect, leaving us to discover the enigma's secret.

Furthermore, there is also a third aspect to be occasionally taken into account, which increases the difficulty. This arises from the practice of some 'urafa' - at least those called the Malamatiyyah - who adopted an inverted form of ostentation (riya' ma'kus) in their discourses by cultivating ill fame instead of good name and fame amongst the people. This means that as opposed to those afflicted with the vice of ostentation (riya') who wish to make themselves appear better than they actually are, the 'urafa' practising self-reproach seek to be considered good by God and yet appear to the people as bad. In this way they seek to cure themselves of all types of ostentation and egoism.

It is said that the majority of the 'urafa' of Khurasan were Malamatiyyah. Some even believe that Hafiz was one. Such words as rindi (libertinism), la ubaligari (carelessness); qalandari (mendicancy), qallashi (pauperism) and the like signify indifference to creation, not to the Creator. Hafiz has spoken a lot on the subject of giving the impression of doing things that earn for one a bad name, while being inwardly good and righteous. A few examples:

If an adherent of the path of love, worry not about bad name. The Shaykh-e San'an had his robe in pawn at a gambling house. Even if I mind the reproaches of claimants, My drunken libertinism would leave me not. The asceticism of raw libertines is like a village path, But what good would the thought of reform do to one of worldwide ill fame like me? Through love of wine I brought my self-image to naught, In order to destroy the imprint of self-devotion. How happily passes the time of a mendicant, who in his spiritual journey, Keeps reciting the Name of the Lord, while playing with the beads of his pagan rosary. However, Hafiz, elsewhere condemns the ostentatious cultivation of ill fame just as he condemns sanctimoniousness:

My heart, let me guide thee to the path of salvation: Neither boast of your profligacy, nor publicize your piety. Rumi defends the Malamatiyyah in the following verses:

Behold, do not despise those of bad name, Attention must be given to their secrets. How often gold has been painted black, For the fear of being stolen and lost. This issue is one of those over which the fuqaha' have found fault with the 'urafa'. Just as Islamic law condemns sanctimony (riya') - considering it a form of shirk - so does it condemn this seeking of reproach. It says that a believer has no right to compromise his social standing and honour. Many 'urafa' also condemn this practice.

In any case, this practice, which has been common amongst some 'urafa', led them to wrap their ideas in words which conveyed the very opposite of what they meant. Naturally this makes the understanding of their intentions a good deal harder.

Abu al-Qasim Qushayri, one of the leading figures of 'irfan, declares in his Risalah that the 'urafa' intentionally speak in enigmas, for they do not want the uninitiated to become aware of their customs, states and their aims. This, he tells us, is because they are incapable of being understood by the uninitiated.[19]

The technical terms of 'irfan are many. Some of them are related to theoretical 'irfan, that is to say, to the mystic world-view and its ontology. These terms resemble the terms of philosophy and are relatively recent. The father of all or most of them was Ibn al-'Arabi. It is extremely difficult to understand them. Amongst these are fayd al-'aqdas (the holiest grace), fayd al-muqaddas (the holy grace), al-wujud al-munbasit (the extending existence), haqq makhluq bi hadarat al-khams, maqam al-'ahadiyyah (the station of uniqueness), maqam al-wahidiyyah (the station of oneness), and so on.

The others are related to practical 'irfan, i.e. the sayr wa suluk of 'irfan. These terms, being of necessity related to the human being, are similar to the concepts of psychology and ethics. In fact they are part of a special type of psychology, a psychology that is indeed empirical and experimental. According to the 'urafa', philosophers - and for that matter psychologists, theologians and sociologists, let alone another class of scholars - who have not entered this valley to observe and study the self at close hand, have no right to make judgements on this subject.

The terms of practical 'irfan, as opposed to those of theoretical 'irfan, are ancient. They can be dated as early as the 3rd/9th century, from the time of Dhu al-Nun, Ba Yazid and Junayd. Here follows an exposition of some of these terms, according to definitions ascribed to them by Qushayri and others.

1. Waqt (Moment):

In the previous section we came across this word in a passage from Ibn Sina. Now let us turn to the 'urafa's definitions of it. The summary of what Qushayri has to say on this subject is that the concept of waqt is relative. Each state or condition that befalls the 'arif requires of him a special behavioural response. The particular state which calls for a particular kind of behaviour is termed the Moment of a particular 'arif.

Of course, another 'arif in the same state may have a different Moment, or the same 'arif in other circumstances may have a different Moment that will require of him a different behaviour and a different responsibility.

An 'arif must be familiar with these Moments; that is, he must recognize each state that descends upon him from the unseen, as well as the responsibilities which accompany it. The 'arif must also count his Moment as precious. Thus it is said that "the 'arif is the son of the Moment". Rumi says:

The sufi is to be the son of the Moment, O friend; Saying 'tomorrow ' is not a convention of the Way.The Arabic waqt has the same sense as dam (breath) and 'aysh-e naqd (cash of life or cash pleasure) of Persian poetry. Hafiz especially makes much mention of 'the cash of life' and 'counting the moment as precious.' Some of those who are either uninformed or who wish to exploit Hafiz as an excuse for their own perverseness, suppose or pretend that Hafiz's use of such words is an invitation to material pleasures and indifference to the cares of the future, to the Hereafter and God - an attitude which is known in the West as Epicureanism.

The notions of 'counting the moment as precious' or 'ready pleasure' is of the recurring motifs of Hafiz's poetry. Perhaps he mentions it thirty times or more. It is obvious that since in his poetry Hafiz observes the 'urafa's practice of speaking in enigmas and symbols, many of his ambiguous verses may appear, on the surface, to present perverse ideas. In order to clear away any such delusions, one may count the following verses as throwing light on others like them.

Whether I drink wine or not, what have I to do with anyone? I am the guard of my secrets and gnostic of my moment. Get up, let's take the sufi's cloak to the tavern, And the theopathetic ravings to the bazaar of nonsense; Let's be ashamed of these polluted woolens, If the name of miracle be given to this virtue and skill; If the heart fails to value the moment and does nothing, Now much shame will the moments bring in for us.In a land, at morning time, a wayfarer Said this to a companion on the way, O sufi, the wine becomes pure When it remains in its bottle for forty days. God is disdainful of that woolen cloak a hundred times That has a hundred idols up its sleeve; I see not the joy of 'aysh in anyone, Nor the cure of a heart nor care for religion; The inners have become gloomy, perhaps perchance, A lamp may be kindled by some recluse. Neither the memorizer is alone (with God) during lessons, Nor the scholar enjoys any knowledge of certainty.Hafiz's ambiguous verses on this subject are many. For example:

Grab the pleasure of the moment, for Adam did not tarry More than a moment in the garden of Paradise.Qushayri states that what is meant by the sufi being the 'son of his Moment' is that he performs whatever has upmost priority for him in the 'state' (hal) he is in; and what is meant by 'the Moment is a sharp sword' is that the requirement (hukm) of each Moment is cutting and decisive; to fail to meet it is fatal.

2 & 3. Hal (State) and Maqam (Position):

Well-known amongst the terms of 'irfan are hal (state) and maqam (position). The State is that which descends upon the 'arif's heart regardless of his will, while his Position is that which he earns and attains through his efforts. The State quickly passes but the Position is lasting. It is said that the States are like flashes of lightning that quickly vanish. Hafiz says:

A lightning flash from Layla's house at dawn, Goodness knows, what it did to the love-torn heart of Majnun. And Sa'di says:

Someone asked of he who had lost his son, O enlightened soul, O wise old man, All the way from Egypt you smelt his shirt, Why could you not see him in the well of Canaan. Said he, my State is like a lightning flash, A moment it's there, another moment gone; Often it lifts me to the highest sky, And often I see not what is at my feet. Should a dervish in his State persist, The two worlds will lie in his hands. Above we have already quoted the following sentence from the Nahj al-balaghah which is relevant here too:

He has revived his intellect and slain his self, until his (bodily and spiritual) bulkiness shrunk and his coarseness turned into tenderness. Then an effulgence, like brilliant flash of lightning, shone into his heart and illuminated the path before him.... (Nahj al-balaghah, Khutab, No. 220, p. 337) The 'urafa' call these flashes lawa'ih, lawami' and tawali' depending upon their degree of intensity and length of duration.

4 & 5. Qabd (Contraction) and Bast (Expansion):

These two words are also amongst those to which the 'urafa' apply a special meaning, They refer to two contrasting spiritual states of the 'arif's soul; qabd (contraction) refers to a sense of desolation felt by it, while bast (expansion) is a state of expansion and joy. The 'urafa' have discussed these two states and their respective causes extensively.

6 & 7. Jam (Gatheredness) and Farq (Separation):

These two terms are much used by the 'urafa'. According to Qushayri: 'That which is on the part of the creature and acquired by the creature and worthy of the station of creaturehood is called farq; while that which is on the part of God- such as inspiration - is called jam'. He whom God makes halt at the station (maqam) of obedience and worship is at the station of farq; and he upon whom God reveals His favours is at the station of jam'.

Hafiz says:

Listen to me with the ear of awareness and for pleasure strive, For these words came at dawn from the caller unseen; Stop thinking of 'separation ' that you become 'gathered' For, as a rule, the angel enters as soon as the Devil leaves. 8 & 9. Ghaybah (Absence) and Hudur (Presence):

Ghaybah is a state of unawareness of creation that occasionally descends upon the 'arif, in which he forgets himself and his surroundings. The 'arif becomes unaware of himself due to his presence (hudur) before God. In the words of a poet:

I am not so occupied with you, O of heavenly face, For the memories of bygone selfhood still flash within my heart.In this state of 'presence' with God and 'absence' from himself and his surroundings, it is possible that important occurrences take place around him without his becoming aware of them. In this connection the 'urafa' have many famous stories. Qushayri writes that Abu Hafs al-Haddad of Nishabur left his trade as a blacksmith because of one incident. Once as he was busy working in his shop, someone recited a verse of the Holy Quran. This put al-Haddad in a state that rendered him totally heedless of his sensible surroundings. Without realizing it he removed a piece of red-hot iron from the furnace with his bare hand. His apprentice cried out to him and he returned to his senses. Thereupon he gave up that trade.

Qushayri also writes that al Shibli once came to see Junayd while Junayd's wife was also sitting there. Junayd's wife made a movement as if to leave, but Junayd stopped her saying that al-Shibli was in a 'state', and heedless of her. She sat a while. Junayd conversed with al-Shibli for some time until al Shibli slowly began to cry. Junayd then turned to his wife telling her to veil herself for al-Shibli was returning to his senses.

Hafiz says:

As every report that I heard has led to perplexity, From now on it is me, the cupbearer, and the state of heedlessness. If it is presence you want do not be absent from Him, Hafiz When you meet what you desire, abandon the world and forget it.It is along these lines that the 'urafa' explain the states of the awliya' during their prayers, in which they became totally heedless of themselves and of their surroundings. Later we shall see that there is a level higher than 'absence', and it was this that the awliya' were subject to.

10,11,12 & 13. Dhawq, Shurb, Sukr and Riyy:

The 'urafa' believe that mere conceptual knowledge of anything has no attraction; the attractiveness of a thing and the ability to inspire passion is subsequent to 'tasting'. At the end of the eighth section of his al-'Isharat Ibn Sina mentions this; he gives the example of a man who is impotent. He says that however much one may describe sexual pleasure to a person devoid of the sexual instinct, who has never had the taste of this pleasure, he will never be sexually aroused. Thus dhawq is the tasting of pleasure. In the terminology of 'irfan it means the actual perception of the pleasure derived from manifestations (tajalliyat) and revelations (mukashafat). Dhawq is the beginning of this, its continuance is called shurb (drinking), its joy sukr (intoxication) and being satiated with it riyy (thirst-quenching).

The 'urafa' are of the view that whatever is derived from dhawq is 'an appearance of intoxication' (tasakur) and not 'intoxication' (sukr) itself. Intoxication, they say, is obtained from 'drinking' (shurb). That which is obtained by 'becoming quenched' (riyy) is 'sobriety' (sahw), or the return to the senses.

It is in this sense that the 'urafa' have talked much about sharab and mey that would ordinarily mean wine.

14, 15 & 16. Mahw, Mahq, and Sahw:

In the 'urafa's discourses, the words mahw (effacement) and sahw (sobriety) are very common. What is meant by mahw is that the 'arif reaches such a stage that his ego becomes effaced in the Divine Essence.

He no more perceives his own ego as others do. And if this effacement reaches such a point that the effects of his ego are also effaced, they call this mahq (obliteration). Mahw and mahq are both higher than the stage of ghaybah, as indicated above. Mahw and mahq mean fana' (annihilation). Yet it is possible for an 'arif to return from the state of fana' to the state of baqa' (abiding in God). It does not however, mean a retrogression from a higher state; rather it means that the 'arif finds subsistence in God. This state, loftier even than mahw and mahq, is called sahw.

17. Khawatir (Thoughts):

The 'urafa' call the thoughts and inspirations cast into their hearts waridat (arrivals). These waridat are sometimes in the form of states of 'contraction' or 'expansion', joy or sadness, and sometimes in the form of words and speech. In the latter case they are called khawatir (sing. khatirah). It is as if someone inside him is speaking to the 'arif.

The 'urafa' have much to say on the subject of khawatir. They say that they can be rahmani (i.e. from God), shaytani (inspired by the Devil) or nafsani (musings of the self). The khawatir constitute one of the dangers of the path, for it is possible that due to some deviation or error the Devil may come to dominate the human being. In the words of the Quran:

Verily the satans inspire their friends ... (6:121) They say that the more adept should be able to discern whether the khatirah is from God or from the Devil. The fundamental criterion is to see what a particular khatirah commands or prohibits; if its command or prohibition is contrary to the dicta of the Shari'ah, then it is definitely satanic. The Quran says:

Shall I inform you upon whom the Satans descend ? They descend upon every lying, sinful one. (26:221-222)18.,19. & 20. Qalb, Ruh and Sirr:

The 'urafa' have different words for the human soul; sometimes they call it nafs (self), sometimes qalb (heart), sometimes ruh (spirit) and sometimes sirr (mystery). When the human soul is dominated and ruled by desires and passions they call it nafs. When it reaches the stage of bearing Divine knowledge, it is called qalb. When the light of Divine love dawns within it, they call it ruh. And when it reaches the stage of shuhud, they call it sirr. Of course, the 'urafa' believe in levels beyond this, which they call khafi (the 'hidden') and akhfa (the 'most hidden').

Notes:

1. Murtada Mutahhari, An Introduction to Ilm al Kalam, transl. By Ali Quli Qarai, Al-Tawhid, vol II No. 2

2. R.A Nicholson, Mysticism in The Legacy of Islam, London 1931 ed. by Sir Thomas Arnold and Alfred Guillaume pp. 211-212

3. Ibid

4. Ibid

5. Dr Qasim Ghani, Tarikh e Tasawwuf Dar Islam, p. 19

6. Farid al Din al Attar, Tadhkirat al-awliya

7. Abu Nasr al Sarraj, al-Luma, p. 427

8. Dr. Qasim Ghani, op. cit

9. Abbas al Qummi, Safinat al Bihar, under s-l-m

10. Harith al Muhasibi, not Hasan al Basri

11. Nicholson, op cit p. 214

12. Dr. Qasim Ghani, op cit p. 462

13. Ibid, p. 55

14. Abu Abd al Rahman al Sulami, Tabqat al sufiyyah, p. 206

15. Authors work Ilal e girayeh be maddehgari

16. Can't find

17. Hafiz is the most beloved figure of Persian poetry in Iran

18. Ahmad Jami was known as Shaykh al Isma

19. al-Qushayri, Risalah, p. 33

Chapter 3

Part 2: by Allamah Husayn Tabatabai - Stages of Spiritual Journey

Allamah Muhammad Husayn Tabatabai

A materialist passes his life in the dark valley of materialism. He is plunged in the sea of evil desires and always is tossed from this side to that side by the waves of material relations of wealth, wife and children. He cries for help, but in vain and in the end gets nothing but disappointment.

Sometimes in this sea a breath of enlivening breeze (divine impulse) pats him and kindles in him a hope that he may reach the shore safely. But this breeze does not blow regularly. It is only occasional.

"In your life you get some pleasant breaths from your Lord. Make a point of being benefited by them and do not turn away from them."

Under the divine impulse the novice decides to somehow or other pass the world of plurality This journey is called by the gnostics sayr wa suluk (spiritual journey).

Suluk means to traverse the path and sayr means to view the characteristics and prominent features of the stages and stations on the way.

Riyazat and acts of self-mortification are the provisions required for this spiritual journey. As it is not easy to renounce the material relations, the novice slowly breaks the snares of the world of plurality and cautiously begins his journey from the material world.

Before long he enters another world called "barzakh". This is the world of his evil desires and inner thoughts. Here he finds that material relations have accumulated a lot of impurities in his heart. These impurities which are an offshoot of his material relations, are a product of his voluptuous thoughts and sensual desires.

These thoughts obstruct the novice in the pursuit of his spiritual journey with a result that he loses peace of mind. He wants to enjoy the recollection of Allah for some time, but these thoughts suddenly interrupt him

60

and foil his efforts

Somebody has well said that man is always engrossed in his petty thoughts and haunted by the ideas of gain and loss. As a result he not only loses his composure and peace of mind, but can also not pay attention to his spiritual journey to a higher world. It is obvious that mental unrest is more harmful than any physical loss or pain. Man can avoid the clash of external relations and interests, but it is difficult for him to get rid of his own ideas and thoughts because they are always with him.

Anyhow, the true seeker of Allah and traveler in his way is not distressed and discouraged by these obstacles and continues to boldly proceed to his destination with the help of his divine impulse, till he safely gets out of the world of petty and conflicting ideas called barzakh. He has to be very vigilant and watchful lest any vicious thought may remain lurking in some hidden corner of his mind.

When these vicious thoughts are turned out, they usually hide in some hidden corner of the mind. The poor spiritual traveler wrongly thinks that he has got rid of their mischief, but when he has found the way to the fountain of life and wants to drink from it, they suddenly appear to ruin him.

This spiritual traveler may be compared to a person who has built a water tank in his house but has not used long. In the meantime the impurities and pollution have settled down in the bottom of the tank although water appears to be clear from above. He thinks that water is clean, but when he gets down into the tank or washes something in it, black patches appear on the surface and he finds that water is dirty.

For this reason it is necessary for the sālik (spiritual traveler) to concentrate his thoughts with the help of riyāzat and acts of self-mortification so that his attention may not be diverted from Allah. At last when after passing through the barzakh the spiritual traveler enters the spiritual world, he still has to traverse several more stages the details of which we will describe later.

In short the spiritual traveler watching his own lower self and the Divine Names and Attributes gradually advances till ultimately he reaches the stage of total fanā (self-annihilation) that is passing away from his own perishable will and then the station of baqā (abiding in the everlasting Will of Allah). It is at this stage that the secret of eternal life is revealed to him.

We can infer this doctrine from the Holy Qur'an also if we ponder over certain verses of it.

Think not of those who are slain in the way of Allah, as dead. Nay, they are living. With their Lord they have provisions. (Surah Āli Imran, 3: 169).

Everything will perish save His Countenance.1 (28:88)

That which you have is wasted away, and that which is with Allah remains. (Surah an Nahl, 6:96)

These verses put together show that the countenance of Allah are those "who are living and who have provisions with their Lord." According to the text of Qur'an they never perish. Certain other verses indicate that the countenance of Allah signifies Divine names which are imperishable. In one of its verses the Qur'an itself has interpreted the Countenance as the Divine names and characterizes the Countenance of Allah as of glory and honor: Everyone who is living will pass away, and there will remain the countenance of your Lord of glory and honor (Surah ar Rahmān, 55:27)

All the commentators of the Qur'an agree that in this verse the phrase "of glory and honor" qualifies the countenance, and it means the countenance of glory and honor. As we know, the countenance of everything is that which manifests it. The manifestations of Allah are His Names and Attributes. It is through them that the creation looks at Allah, or in other words, knows Him. With this explanation we come to the conclusion that every existing thing perishes and wastes away except the glorious and beautiful names of Allah. This also shows that the gnostics to whom the verse, "Nay, they are living and have their provisions with their Lord", applies, are the manifestations of the glorious and beautiful Names of Allah.

From the above it is also clear what the Holy Imams meant when they said: "We are the Names of Allah." Obviously to be the head of a government or to be the highest religious and legal authority is not a position which could be described by these words. What actually these words denote is the state of passing away in Allah, abiding permanently with His countenance and being a manifestation of His glorious and beautiful Names and Attributes.

In connection with the spiritual journey another important and essential thing is meditation or contemplation (muraqabah). It is necessary for the spiritual traveler not to ignore meditation at any stage from the beginning to the end. It must be understood that meditation has many grades and is of many types. In the initial stages the spiritual traveler has to do one type of meditation and at later stages of another type. As the spiritual traveler goes forward, his meditation becomes so strong that if ever it was undertaken by a beginner, he would either give it up for good or would be mad. But after successfully completing the preliminary stages, the gnostic becomes able to undertake the higher stages of meditation. At that time many things which were lawful to him in the beginning get forbidden to him.

As a result of careful and diligent meditation a flame of love begins to kindle in the heart of the spiritual traveller, for it is an inborn instinct of man to love the Absolute Beauty and Perfection. But the love of material things overshadows this inherent love and does not allow it to grow and become visible.

Meditation weakens this veil till ultimately it is totally lifted. Then that innate love appears in its full splendour and leads man's conscience towards Allah. The mystic poets often figuratively call this divine love "wine".

When the gnostic continues to undertake meditation, for quite a long time, divine divine lights begin to be visible to him. In the beginning these lights flash like lightning for a moment and then disappear. Gradually the divine lights grow strong and appear like little stars. When they grow further, they appear first like the moon and then like the sun. Sometimes they appear like a burning lamp also. In the gnostic terminology these lights are known as the gnostic sleep and they belong to the world of barzakh.

When the spiritual traveler has passed this stage and his meditation grows stronger, he sees as if the heaven and the earth were all illuminated from the East to the West. This light is called the light of self and is seen after the gnostic has passed the world of barzakh. When after coming out of the world of barzakh primary manifestations of self begin to occur, the spiritual traveler views himself in a material form. He often feels that he is standing beside himself. This stage is the beginning of the stage of self stripping.

Allamah Mirza Ali Qāzi used to say that one day when he came out from his room into the veranda he suddenly saw himself standing quietly beside himself. When he looked carefully, he saw that there was no skin or flesh on his face. He went back into his room and looked into the mirror. He found his face was as empty as it had never been.

Sometimes it happens that the gnostic feels as if he did not exist at all. He tries to find himself but he does not succeed. These the observations of the early stages of self-stripping, but they are not free from the limitations of time and space. In the next stage, with Allah's help the spiritual traveler can rise above these limitations also and can view complete reality of his self. It is reported that Mirza Jawad Malaki Tabrizi passed full fourteen years in Akhund Mulla Husayn Quli Hamdani's company and took from him lessons in gnosis. He says:

"One day my teacher told me about one of his pupils that thence forward his training was my responsibility. This pupil was very pains-taking and diligent. For six years he kept himself busy with meditation and self-mortification. At last he reached the stage of knowing his self and having been stripped of his evil self (passion and lust). I deemed it proper that the teacher himself should tell that fact to this pupil. So I took him to the house of the teacher whom I told what I wanted. The teacher said: "That's nothing." At the same time he waved his hand and said: "This is stripping." That pupil used to say: "I saw myself being stripped of my body and at the same time felt as if another person just like me was standing beside me."

It may be mentioned here that to see the things existing in the world of barzakh is comparatively of small account. It is of greater significance to view one's own lower self (nafs) in an absolutely stripped state, for in this case self appears as a pure reality free from the limitations of time and space The viewing of the earlier stages was comparatively preliminary and partial and this viewing is so to say the perception of the whole.

Agha Sayyid Ahmad Karbalā'i, another well-known and prominent pupil of the late Akhund says: "One day I was sleeping somewhere when all of a sudden somebody awakened me and said to me: 'Get up at once if you want to see the 'eternal light.' I opened my eyes and saw an immensely bright light shining everywhere and in all directions."

This is a stage of the enlightenment of self. It appears in the shape of an infinite light.

When a lucky spiritual traveler has passed this stage, he passes other stages also with a speed in proportion to the attention he pays to meditation. He views Allah's Attributes or becomes conscious of Allah's Names as an absolute quality. On this occasion he suddenly feels that all existing things are only a unit of knowledge and there exists nothing but one single power. This is the stage of the vision of the Divine attributes. The stage of the vision of Divine names is still higher. At this stage the devotee sees that in all the worlds there exists only one Knower and only one Omnipotent and Living Being. This stage is far higher than that of the consciousness of the Divine Attributes, a state which appears in the heart, for now the spiritual traveler does not find any being knowing, powerful and living except Allah. This degree of vision is usually achieved during the recitation of the Qur'an, when the reader feels that there is somebody else who is listening to his recitation.

It may be remembered that recitation of the Qur'an is very effective in securing this state. The devotee should offer the night prayers and should recite in them those surahs during the recitation of which prostration is obligatory, namely Surah Sajdah, Surah Hāmim Sajdah, Surah Najm, and Surah al-'Alaq, for it is very pleasant to fall prostrating while reciting a surah. Experience has also proved that it is very effective for this purpose to recite the Surah Sād in the Thursday night prayers (wutairah). This characteristic of this surah is indicated by the report concerning the merits of this surah also.

When the devotee has completed all these stages and visions, he is surrounded by divine impulses and every moment he goes closer to the stage of real self-annihilation, till he is so seized by a divine impulse that he is totally absorbed in the beauty and perfection of the "True Beloved." He no longer pays heed to himself or to anybody else. He beholds Allah everywhere. There was Allah and nothing was with Him.

In this condition the devotee is plunged in the fathomless sea of divine vision.

It must be remembered that this does not mean that everyhing in the material world loses its existence. Actually the devotee sees unity in plurality. Otherwise everything continues to exist as it is. A gnostic has said: "I was among the people for 30 years They were under the impression that I was taking part in all their activities but actually throughout this period I did not see them and did not know anyone but Allah."

The coming about of this state is of great importance. In the beginning it may come about only for a moment, but gradually its duration grows longer, first it may last for about 10 minutes or so, then for an hour and subsequently even for a longer period. This state may even become permanent by the grace of Allah.

In the sayings of the gnostics this state has been termed as "abiding in Allah" or "the ever-lasting life in Allah". Man cannot attain to this stage of perfection unless he passes away from self. On attaining to this stage the devotee does not see anything except Allah.

It is said that there was an enraptured sufi who was seized by a divine impulse. His name was Bābā Farajullah. People asked him to say something about the world. He said: "What can I say about it? I have not seen it since I was born."2

In the beginning when the vision is weak, it is called a state and its occurrence is beyond the control of the devotee. But when as a result of continued meditation and by the grace of Allah this state becomes a permanent feature, then it is called a station. Now the state of vision gets under the control of the spiritual traveler or devotee.

Obviously a strong spiritual traveler is he who along with viewing these states keeps an eye to the world of plurality also and maintains well his relations to the world of unity and to the world of plurality at the same time. This is a very high position and cannot be attained easily. Perhaps this position is reserved for the Prophets and some other chosen people who are favorites of Allah and who can say: "The state of my relation to Allah is such that the most favorite angel cannot attain to it."3 and at the same time declare: "I am a human being just like you." 4

Somebody may say that only the Prophets and the Imams can attain to these high positions. How is it possible for others to attain to them? Our reply is that Prophethood and Imamate are undoubtedly the special assignments to which others cannot reach. But the station of 'absolute Oneness' and passing away in Allah which is called wilāyat is not exclusively reserved for the Prophets and the Imams, who have themselves called upon their followers to try to attain to this station of perfection. The Holy Prophet has asked his Ummah (Muslim nation) to follow in his footsteps. This shows that it is possible for others also to advance to this position, or else such an instructions would have no meaning.

The Qur'an says: Surely in the Messenger you have a good example for him who looks to Allah and the Last Day, and remembers Allah much. (Surah al-Ahzāb, 33:21)

There is a report in the Sunni books that once the Holy Prophet said: "Had you not been talkative and of uneasy hearts you would have seen what I see and would have heard what I hear."

This report shows that the real cause of not attaining to human perfection is fiendish thoughts and vicious acts. According to a report from the Shi'ah source also, the Holy Prophet has said: "Had not the satans been roaming around their hearts, the human beings would have seen the whole kingdom of the heavens and the earth."

One of the characteristics of this high human position is that it enables the individual holding it to comprehend the divine kingdoms according to his capacity. He gains the knowledge of the past and the future of the universe and can dominate and control everything, everywhere.

The famous gnostic, Shaykh Abdul Karim al-Jili writes in his book, the 'Perfect Man' that once he was overcome by such a condition that he felt as if he had been unified with all other existing things and could see everything. This state did not last more than a moment.

Obviously it is because of the devotees' preoccupation with their physical needs that this state does not last long.

A well known sufi says that a man gets rid of the traces of material development only 500 years after his death. This period is equivalent to half a day of the divine days. Allah has said: Surely a day with your Lord is like one thousand years of your reckoning. (Surah al-Hajj, 22:47)

It is evident that the next worldly blessings and divine bounties and favors are innumerable and unlimited. The words expressing them have been coined on the basis of human needs and new words need to be coined with the expansion of human requirements. That is why it is not possible to express all divine truths and favors by words. Whatever has been said is only symbolical and metaphorical. It is impossible to express the higher truths in words. It has been said: "You are in the darkest world." According to this tradition man is living in the darkest of the worlds (earth) created by Allah.

Man coins words to meet his daily requirements on the basis of what he sees and feels in this material world. He has no knowledge of the relations, blessings and spirits of the other worlds and, therefore, he cannot coin words for them. That is why there do not exist proper words in any language of the world which may express higher truths and concepts. Now when our knowledge is limited and our thinking faulty, how can this problem be solved?

There are two groups of people who have talked about higher truths. The first is that of the Prophets. They have direct contact with the non-material worlds, but they also say: "We, the Prophets, have been ordered to talk to the people according to their intellectual capacity." That means that they are compelled to express the truths in a way intelligible to the common people. Therefore they have avoided to describe the nature of the spiritual lights and their brilliance. They have not talked about the truths unintelligible to man. They have only used such words as paradise, houries and palaces for the truth about which it has been said: "No eye has seen, no ear has heard and no one has thought about it". They have even admitted that the truths of the other worlds are indescribable.

The second group is of those who advance along the path prescribed by the Prophets and perceive the truths according to their capability. They also use a figurative style.

Sincerity of Devotion

It must be remembered that without being sincere in the way of Allah it is not possible to attain to spiritual stations and stages. Truth cannot be unraveled to a spiritual traveler unless he is fully sincere and single-minded in his devotion.

There are two stages of sincerity. The first stage is of carrying out all religious injunctions for the sake of Allah only. The second stage is of devoting one's entire self exclusively to Allah. The first stage is indicated by the following verse:

They are ordained nothing but to worship Allah keeping religion pure for Him. (Surah al-Bayyinah, 98:5)

The second stage is indicated by the following verse:

Save single minded slaves of Allah. (Surah as Saffat, 37:128)

There is a well known Prophetic tradition to the effect that he who has kept himself pure for Allah for 40 days, fountains of wisdom flow from his heart to his tongue.

This tradition also alludes to the second stage of sincerity. The Qur'an has at certain places described a deed as salih (virtuous and pious). For example it said: "Whoever did a salih (virtuous and pious) deed", And at some other places it describes some men as salih. For example at one place it says: "Surely he was one of the salih (pious)." Similarly it has sometimes described a deed as sincere and sometimes a man as sincere. It is obvious that man's sincerity depends on his deeds and he cannot be sincere unless he is sincere in all his deeds and in all that he does or says. Allah says: "To Him ascends good word and the good deed raises it. (Surah al-Fatir, 35:10)

It may be remembered that a man who attains to the grade of personal sincerity, is endowed with certain other characteristic qualities which are not possessed by others.

An important characteristic which he acquires according to a text of the Qur'an he becomes immune from the domination of Satan. The Qur'an quotes Satan as saying: My Lord, I swear by Your honor, I shall adorn the path of error for them in the earth and shall mislead all of them, except such of them as are your sincerely devoted slaves. (Surah al-Hijr, 38:82)

It is clear that Allah's sincerely devoted slaves have been excluded here not because Satan was forced by Allah to do so. They have been excluded because owing to their attaining to the station of 'unity', Satan can no longer gain control over them. As these people made themselves pure for Allah, they see Allah wherever they cast their eyes. Whatever shape Satan may assume, they see the manifestation of Allah's glory in it. That is why Satan has admitted from the beginning his helplessness against them. Otherwise, it is his job to seduce the children of Adam and to lead them astray. He can have no mercy on anyone.

The second point is that the sincerely devoted slaves of Allah will be exempted from reckoning on the Day of Judgement. The Qur'an says: And the trumpet is blown and all who are in the heavens and the earth swoon away save him whom Allah wills. (Surah az-Zumar, 39:68)

This verse definitely shows that an unspecified group of people will be saved from the horrors of the Day of Judgement. When we match this verse with another verse which reads:

They will surely be produced save sincerely single-minded people, (Surah as Saffat, 37:39 - 40) it becomes clear what that group will be. The sincerely devoted people need not be brought up for reckoning. They have already secured eternal life as the result of their meditations, self-annihilation and ceaseless acts of devotion. They have already passed the reckoning and judgement and as having been slain in the way of Allah, they have provision with their Lord.

Think not of those who are slain in the way of Allah as dead. Nay, they are living. With their Lord they have provision (Surah Ali Imran 3:169)

Moreover, only that one is produced who is not present. These people are already present even before the beginning of the Day of resurrection, for Allah says that they have a provision with their Lord.

The third point is that on the Day of Judgement people will generally be rewarded and recompensed for their deeds. But these sincerely single-minded people will be favored with rewards beyond their deeds. Allah says: You are not requited but what you did, save sincerely single-minded slaves of Allah. (Surah az-Zumar, 39:40)

If it is claimed that this verse means only that the sinners will be punished for their sins, but the reward given to the virtuous will purely be a favour bestowed on them by Allah, we will say that this verse is general in its connotation and does not exclusively refer to the sinners. Moreover, there is no contradiction between Allah's favour and His recompense, for Allah's favor means that He sometimes rewards a great deal for small deeds. In spite of this kind of favor the reward still remains for the deeds performed. But what this verse says is quite a different thing. It says that what Allah will bestow on His sincerely single-minded slaves, will be a pure favor, not a reward for any deeds at all.

Another verse says: There they have all that they desire and there is more with Us (Surah Qaf, 50:35)

This verse means that the inmates of Paradise will have all that man can desire or wish Not only that, but Allah will bestow on them what they cannot imagine or think of. This point is worth considering.

The fourth point is that this group holds such a high position that its members can glorify Allah in the most appropriate manner.

Allah says: Glorified be Allah from what they attribute to Him, except what the sincerely single-minded slaves of Allah say of Him (Surah as - Saffat, 37:159 - 160)

This is the highest position that a man can occupy.

The above mentioned details show what the blessings of this last stage of gnosis are. But it must be kept in mind that these blessings can be obtained only when a spiritual traveler's ceaseless devotion reaches the stage of self-annihilation so that he may be called to have been slain in the way of Allah and may become eligible for the reward reserved for martyrs. Just as in the battlefield the sword cuts off the connection between the body and soul of a martyr, similarly a spiritual traveler snaps off the connection between his body and soul by fighting against his appetitive soul. For this purpose he acquires the help of his spiritual power instead of using his physical force.

In the beginning of his spiritual journey a devotee should lead an ascetic life and should constantly contemplate on the worthlessness of the vanities of the world and thus should break off his relation to the world of plurality. When he would cease to be interested in the world, no material gain will ever please him nor will any material loss grieve him.

So that you grieve not for what you have missed and exult not for what you have been given. (Surah al-Hadid, 57:23)

Indifference to the happiness and sorrow does not mean that the spiritual traveler does not feel happy even about the bounties of Allah or does not grieve at anything which may distress Him, for happiness about Allah's favors is not the result of his love for worldly trivialities such as wealth, rank, honor, fame etc. He loves the bounties of Allah because he finds himself overwhelmed by His mercy.

After passing this stage the devotee feels that he still loves himself ardently. Whatever spiritual effort and exercises he makes is the result of his self-love. Man is selfish by nature. He is always ready to sacrifice everything else for his own self. He would be willing to destroy anything for the sake of his own survival. It is difficult for him to do away with this natural instinct and to overcome his selfishness. But so long as he does not do so, he cannot expect the divine light to manifest itself in his heart. In other words unless a spiritual traveler annihilates his individual self he cannot establish his connection with Allah. Therefore it is necessary for him first to weaken and ultimately to smash the spirit of selfishness so that whatever he may do, is done purely for the sake of Allah and his sense of self-love may turn into love for Him.

For this purpose ceaseless effort is necessary. After passing this stage the devotee's attachment not only to his body and every other thing material ceases to exist, but even his attachment to his soul is finished. Now whatever he does, he does for Allah alone. If he eats to satiate his hunger or provides for the bare necessities of life, he does so only because his Eternal Beloved wants him to continue to live. All his wishes become subject to the Will of Allah. That is why he does not seek any miraculous power for himself. He believes that he has no right to undertake any sort of spiritual exercise with a view to know the past or predict future events or to practice thought-reading or to cover very long distances in a very short time or to make any changes in the universal system or to invigorate his libidinous faculties, for such acts are not performed for pleasing Allah, nor can they be motivated by sincere devotion to Him. They mean only self-worship and are performed for the satisfaction of one's licentious desires, although the person concerned may not admit this fact and although he may apparently be sincerely devoted to Allah. But according to the following verse he only worships his desire. Have you seen him who makes his desire his god? (Surah al-Jathiyah, 45:23)

Therefore the spiritual traveler should pass all these stages cautiously and do his best to gain complete control over his vanity. We shall further talk on this subject later.

When a devotee reaches this final stage, he gradually begins to lose interest in himself and ultimately forgets himself totally. Now he sees nothing except the eternal everlasting beauty of his True Beloved.

It must be borne in mind that it is essential for the spiritual traveler to gain complete victory over the fiendish horde of licentious desires, love for wealth, fame and power, pride and conceit. It is not possible to attain perfection if any trace of self-love is left, that is why it has been observed that many a distinguished man even after years long spiritual exercise and ceaseless acts of devotion could not attain perfection in gnosis and was defeated in his battle against his phenomenal self. The reason was that his heart was not fully purified, and petty desires still lurked in some corner of his heart, though he was under the impression that all his evil qualities had been uprooted. The result was that at the time of test the suppressed desires once again raised their head and began to thrive, with the result that the poor devotee fell on evil times.

Success against the lower self depends on the favor of Allah and cannot be achieved without His help.

It is said that one day the late Bahrul 'Ulum was very cheerful. On being asked about the reason of that, he said: "After performing ceaseless acts of devotion for 25 years now I find my deeds free from ostentation." The lesson in this story is worth being remembered well.

It is to be remembered that a spiritual traveler must abide by the Islamic injunctions from the very beginning of his embarking on the path of gnosis to the end of it. Even the slightest digression from the law is not allowed. If you find that anyone inspite of claiming to be a gnostic, does not follow all the rules of Islamic law and is not strictly pious and virtuous, he may be regarded as a hypocrite and impostor. But if he commits a mistake and has some valid reason to justify his wrong action, then it is a different thing.

It is a big lie and calumny to hold that the Islamic code of law may be disregarded by a wali (Muslim saint). The Holy Prophet held the highest position among all living beings, but he still abided by the injunctions of Islam till the last moments of his life. Therefore it is absolutely wrong to say that a wali is not obligated to observe the law. Anyhow, it is possible to say that an ordinary man worships Allah in order to consummate his potentialities, but a wali worships Him because his high position requires him to do so. Aisha is reported to have said to the Holy Prophet: "When Allah has said about you: So that Allah may forgive you of your sin, that which is past and that which is to come, (Surah al-Fath, 48:2) then why do you exert yourself so much to perform the acts of worship?" The Holy Prophet said: "Should I not be a thankful slave of Allah?"

This shows that certain individuals worship Allah not for the consummation of their personality, but to show their gratitude to Allah.

The states which a spiritual traveler experiences and the lights which he beholds, should be a prelude to his acquisition of certain traits and qualities. Otherwise a simple change in his condition is not enough. The spiritual traveler must completely get rid of all remnants of the lower world in himself by means of meditation and ceaseless acts of devotion. It is not possible to acquire the position of the virtuous and the pure without acquiring their qualities. A little slip in the matters of meditation and acts of devotion may cause a spiritual traveler a tremendous loss. The following verse throws light on this point: Muhammad is but a messenger. Other messengers have passed away before him. Will it be that, when he dies or is slain, you will turn back on your heels? (Surah Ali Imran, 3:144)

Therefore the spiritual traveler must cleanse his heart and purify himself inwardly and outwardly so that he may be graced with the company of the pure souls.

Allah says: Forsake outward as well as inward sins. (Surah al-An'am, 6:120)

Acting according to this verse the spiritual traveler must pass all those stages which enable him to arrive at the stage of sincere devotion. These stages have been briefly enumerated in the following verse:

Those who believe, and have left their homes and strive with their wealth and their lives in Allah's way, are of much greater worth in Allah's sight. These are they who are triumphant. Their Lord gives them good tidings of mercy from Him, and acceptance, and Gardens where enduring pleasures will be theirs. There they will abide forever. Surely with Allah there is an immense reward. (Surah at-Tawbah, 9:20-22)

According to this verse there are four worlds preceding to the world of sincere devotion: (i) World of Islam, (ii) World of faith, (iii) World of emigration, and (iv) World of Jihad in the way of Allah. According to the Prophetic tradition in which it has been said: "We have returned from a minor holy war to a major holy war", the spiritual traveler's struggle is a major holy war (major jihad), and as such his Islam also should be a major Islam and his faith also a major faith. After passing the stages of Islam and faith he should muster enough courage to be able to emigrate in the company of the inward messenger with the help of the outward messenger or his successor. Thus he should undertake self-mortification, so that he may gain the status of a person slain in the way of Allah.

The spiritual traveler must keep it in mind that from the beginning of his spiritual journey till the stage of self-mortification he has to face many obstacles, which are created either by man or the Devil. He has to pass through the worlds of major Islam and major faith before reaching the stage of self-mortification and gaining the status of a martyr. In the spiritual journey major Islam, major faith, major emigration and major holy war are preliminary stages preceding the final stage. The major obstacles in the way to these stages are called major infidelity and major hypocrisy. At this stage the junior devils can do no harm to the spiritual traveler, but Satan who is their supreme head still tries to obstruct his progress. Therefore, while passing through these stages he should not think that he is out of danger. So long as he does not pass out of above-mentioned "major worlds", Satan will continue to obstruct his way. The spiritual traveler should keep up his spirit and beware of Satan, lest he be involved in major infidelity or major hypocrisy. After passing through the worlds of major Islam and major faith the spiritual traveler undertakes major emigration and then by means of self-mortification he passes through major self-resurrection and then passes into the valley of those who are sincerely devoted to Allah. May Allah grant us all this success.

Notes:

1. Countenance of Allah signifies the Divine names and attributes through which Allah manifests Himself in all existing things. All things will perish but their countenance will remain because that is the manifestation of Allah. In simpler words it may be said that the 'basis' on which depends the existence of things does not perish.

2. The biography of Baba Faraj, the enraptured is available in Tarikh Hashari. It is about the learned men and the sufis and gnostics of Tabriz. There is a couplet in it regarding the above words of Baba Faraj. There are similar versified sayings of Hāfiz and the renowned Arab mystical poet, ibn Fāriz.

3. A tradition of an Imam.

4. In the Qur'an Allah asks the Holy Prophet to tell the pagans: "I am a human being just like you, except that I receive revelation."

Chapter 4

The Twelve Worlds

Allamah Muhammad Husayn Tabatabai

On the basis of what has been said above, a devotee, making a spiritual journey has to pass through 12 Worlds before reaching the world of sincerity. The names of these worlds are:

minor Islam, major Islam, greater Islam, minor faith, major faith, greater faith, minor emigration, major emigration, greater emigration, minor jihad, major jihad and greater jihad. It is necessary to know the characteristics of these worlds and to be aware of the obstacles and barriers which a devotee has to face while advancing towards them. To make our point clear we describe these worlds briefly.

Major Islam means complete submission to Allah, not to criticize any action of His and to believe with full conviction that what is happening is not without some advantage and what is not happening was not advisable. Imam Ali hints at this point when he says that 'Islam means submission and submission signifies conviction.' A devotee not only should have no objection against any Divine directives or decrees but also should not feel even in his heart unhappy about any of them. Allah says:

But nay, by your Lord, they will not be faithful unless they make you judge of what is in dispute between them and find within themselves no dislike of that which you decide, and submit with full submission. (Surah an-Nisa, 4:65)

This is the stage of greater Islam. At this stage Islam should infiltrate the soul of the devotee and truly overwhelm his heart and life.

When the devotee's heart is illuminated by the light of greater Islam, not only his heart testifies that everything is from Allah, but he also physically observes this truth. In other words, he often sees with the eyes of his heart that Allah is omnipresent and omniscient. This stage is called that of vision and greater Islam. Rut as the spiritual traveller has not yet attained to perfection, he has to face many material obstacles, especially when he is busy with his natural needs, a state of unmindfulness overcomes him. Therefore it is necessary for him to use his will power so that the state of vision may become a permanent feature for him and may not be disturbed by his other activities. For this purpose it is necessary to push the state of greater Islam from the heart to the soul so that this elementary state may become a fully developed state governing all internal and external faculties. This is the stage which is called by the gnostics the station of well doing (ihsan). The Qur'an says: As for those who strive in Us, we surely guide them to Our path. Surely Allah is with those who do well. (Surah al-Ankabut, 29:69)

As such a striver in the way of Allah cannot find the way of guidance and proximity of Allah until he reaches the stages of well doing. An eminent companion of the Holy Prophet Abu Zar Ghifari once asked him what well doing signified. The Holy Prophet said: "That you worship Allah as though you see him. If you do not see Him, He surely sees you". In other words, man should worship Allah as if he was seeing Him. If he is unable to worship Him in this way, then there is a lower grade of worship. He should worship Allah as though Allah was seeing him. So long as the devotee does not reach the stage of greater faith, he is only occasionally invested with the state of well-doing. In this state he performs the acts of worship with zeal and fervor. His soul having been imbued with faith, puts all his organs and faculties on their proper job. The organs and faculties once controlled cannot disobey the soul even for a moment. Concerning the devotees who have attained to the stage of greater faith Allah says: Successful indeed are the believers, who are humble in their prayers and who shun all that is vain. (Surah al-Mu'minun, 23:1-3)

Only that man will busy himself with trivial things who is interested in them. A spiritual traveller who has attained to the stage of greater faith and for whom well doing has become a habit, cannot be fond of anything vain, for no heart can love two contradictory things at one and the same time. Allah Himself has said: Allah has not assigned to any man two hearts within his body. (Surah al-Ahzab, 33:4)

If we find any devotee flittering away his time in amusements, we can easily conclude that he is not fully devoted to Allah and that his heart is not free from the hypocrisy which is called in this context greater hypocrisy and which is the opposite of greater faith. As a result of this hypocrisy man does not act according to his inner incitement, but is guided by reason, expediency or apprehensions. The following verse refers to this kind of hypocrisy: When they stand up to offer prayers, they perform it languidly. (Surah an-Nisa', 4:142)

When the spiritual traveller attains to the stage of greater faith, no trace of hypocrisy is left in him. His actions and deeds are no longer guided by unreliable directives of reason nor by any apprehension, expediency or conservatism. All his actions are then motivated by inner zeal, hearty inclination and real love. Once the spiritual traveller attains to the stage of greater faith, he should be ready for greater emigration. There are two sides of this emigration: one is bodily emigration which means giving up social dealings with the wicked, and the other is emigration of heart which means not making friends with them. A spiritual traveller not only has to abandon all habits, customs and usages which prevent him from pursuing the path of Allah, but has also to dislike them from the core of his heart. Such customs and usages have been mostly imported from the countries of the infidels. A man living in a material society becomes a prisoner of many customs and habits prevalent among the worldly people forming the basis of their social dealings. For example it has become customary to regard a person keeping quiet at an academic discussion as ignorant. Many people consider it a mark of their eminence to sit at the head of a meeting or to go ahead of others while walking in company. Fine talk and flattery are called good manners, and a behaviour contrary to these customs is described as bad manner and vulgarity. The spiritual traveller should with the help of Allah ignore such odd customs and whimsical ideas. In this regard he should not fear anybody and pay no attention even to the criticism of those who call themselves great scholars. There is a report in Kulayni's Jami' on the authority of Imam Ja'far Sadiq that the Holy Prophet has said: "There are four pillars of infidelity: greed, fear, resentment and anger". In this tradition fear means an apprehension that people would be angry if their wrong ideas and wrong customs were opposed.

In short the spiritual traveller should say good-bye to all those habits and traditions, customs and usages which obstruct his advancement towards Allah. The gnostics call this attitude 'madness', because mad people also take little interest in and pay little attention to the popular habits and traditions and do not care what the other people would say. A mad man sticks to his own ways and does not fear any opposition.

Following his success in emigration and getting rid of the prevailing customs, the spiritual traveller enters the field of major jihad, which means a fight against the devilish hordes. Even at this stage the spiritual traveller is still a captive of his lower self, overwhelmed by his passions, and low desires and perplexed by apprehensions and worries, anger and disappointments. If anything that is not to his liking happens, he is upset and feels hurt. In order to overcome all his worries, griefs and pains, the spiritual traveller should seek Divine aid and crush the forces of apprehension, anger and lust. On getting rid of worldly botherations and worries he will enter the world of greater Islam. Then he will feel as if he was prevailing over the whole world, was safe from death and effacement and was free from every kind of conflict. He will find in himself a purity and glamour not connected with this humble world. At this stage the devotee becomes totally unconcerned with this transient world, as if he was dead. Now he begins a new life. He lives in the world of humanity, but sees everything in the shape of the angelic world. Material things can no longer do him any harm. As he has reached the middle stage of self-resurrection, veil is gradually lifted from before his eyes and he can see many hidden things. This station is called that of greater Islam. The Qur'an clearly refers to it in the following words:

Is he who was dead and We have raised him to life, and set for him a light wherein he walks among men, like him who is in utter darkness whence he cannot come out? Thus is their conduct made fair-seeming for the disbelievers. (Surah al-Anfal, 6:122)

Whosoever does right, whether male or female, and is a believer, we shall surely quicken him with good life and We shall pay them a recompense in proportion to the best of what they used to do. (Surah an-Nahl, 16:97)

It should be kept in mind that what the devotee views in this state may create in him a sense of false pride and as a result of that, his worst enemy, that is his lower self may begin to resist him. There is a tradition which says: "The most deadly enemy of yours is your lower self which is within you."

In these circumstances the devotee is in danger of being involved in greater infidelity unless he is helped and protected by Allah. The following tradition refers to this kind of infidelity. "The lower self is the greatest idol". It was this idol-worship for being protected from which the Prophet Ibrahim prayed to Allah when he said: "Save me and my sons from worshipping idol". Evidently it is unimaginable that Prophet Ibrahim would ever worship any fabricated idols. It was this kind of idol-worship from which the Holy Prophet also sought refuge when be said: "Allah, I seek refuge in you from hidden polytheism".

Therefore the devotee should whole-heartedly acknowledge his humbleness and completely do away with the idea of self-conceit from his heart so that he may not commit greater infidelity and may succeed in attaining to greater Islam. Some gnostics have throughout their life avoided even the use of the word 'I'. Some others attributed all that is good to Allah and only what could not be attributed to Allah, they attributed to themselves. They used first person plural pronoun while talking of a thing that could be attributed to themselves and to Allah both. They derived this method from the story of the Prophet Musa and Khizr. Khizr said: As for the boat, it belonged to poor people working on the river, and I wished to mar it, for there was a king behind them who was taking every boat by force. (Surah al-Kahf, 18:79)

As the act of marring could not be attributed to Allah, he attributed it to himself and used a first person singular pronoun.

And as for the lad, his parents were believers and we feared lest he should oppress them by rebellion and disbelief And therefore we intended that their Lord should change him for them for one better in purity and nearer to mercy. (Surah al-Kahf, 18:80-81)

In this case as the act of slaying the lad could be attributed both to Allah and Khizr, the plural pronoun was used.

And as for the wall, it belonged to two orphan boys in the city, and there was beneath it a treasure belonging to them. Their father had been righteous, and your Lord intended that they should come to their full strength and should bring out their treasure as a mercy from their Lord. (Surah al-Kahf, 18:82)

As the intention of doing good to someone is attributable to Allah, it has been attributed to Him.

We find Prophet Ibrahim also employing this style of speech. He said: It is He Who created me and Who does guide me, and who feeds me and waters me, and who heals me when I get sick. (Surah ash-Shu'ara, 26:78-80)

Here Prophet Ibrahim attributes sickness to himself and healing to Allah.

A devotee should leave no stone unturned to attain to the stage of major Islam and to do away with self-conceit.

Haji Imam Quli Nakhjawani was the teacher in gnosis of Agha Sayyid Husayn Agha Qazi, the father of the late Agha Mirza Ali Qazi. He completed his training in morality and gnosis at the hands of Sayyid Quraysh Qazwini. He says that when he got aged, one day he saw that he and Satan were standing on the top of a hill. He passed his hand on his beard and said to Satan: "Now I am an old man please spare me if you can." Satan said: "Look this side." Sayyid Qazwini says that when he looked that side, he saw a ditch so deep that it sent a cold wave into his spine. Pointing to that ditch Satan said: "I have no sympathy or mercy for anybody. If I could lay my hands on you once, you would fall into the bottom of this ditch from which you would never have an escape."

Next to greater Islam is the stage of greater faith, which means such an intense upsurge of major Islam that it may transform the knowledge of truth into a clear view of it, In the meantime the spiritual traveller moving from the angelic world ('Alam Malakut) enters the souled world ('Alam Jabarut). For him greater self-resurrection would have already taken place and he can now see the sights of the souled world.

Thereafter the spiritual traveller should emigrate from his own existence which is to be totally rejected by him. This journey of his will be from his own existence to the absolute existence. Some saints have expressed this idea by saying: "Leave your self and come." The following verses of the Qur'an hint at it: 0 contented soul, return to your Lord in His good pleasure. Enter among My bondmen! Enter My Garden. (Surah al-Fajr, 89:27 - 30). In this verse the soul has been described as contented and addressed as such. It has been asked to join the ranks of the chosen people of Allah and enter the paradise.

The spiritual traveller has now completed the stage of major jihad and entered the world of victory and conquest which is the headquarters of contentment, but as some traces of his existence still remain, he has not yet completed the process of self-annihilation and hence needs embarking on greater jihad. Because of this deficiency he is not yet absolutely free. His place is still in the compound hinted at in the Qur'anic verse, "in the nice sitting place with the Powerful Potentate". (Surah al-Qamar, 54:55) Here 'Powerful Potentate' refers to Allah.

After this stage the spiritual traveller should wage a war against the remaining traces of his existence and remove them completely, so that he may step forward into the field of absolute 'unity'. This world is called the world of victory and conquest. The spiritual traveller has to pass through twelve such worlds before he succeeds in passing the stages of greater emigration and greater jihad and enters the field of sincerity. Then he will be called successful and victorious and will enter the world of sincerity and the compound of We belong to Allah and We will surely return to Him (Surah al-Baqarah, 2:156). For him the greater self-resurrection will already have taken place. He will enter the stage of total passing away from self after crossing the curtains of bodies, souls and every thing fixed and appointed. He will have one foot in the world of divinity, and he will have passed the stage of Everybody has to taste death (Surah Ali Imran, 3:185). Such a person being at the stage of passing away from self though consciously alive, yet in one sense will be dead. That is why concerning Imam Ali the Holy Prophet said: "Whoever wants to see a dead man walking, let him see Ali ibn Abi Talib."

Explanation: The spiritual excellences and their signs and consequences which have been briefly mentioned above, are the favors which have been bestowed by Allah exclusively on the followers of the Last Prophet, Muhammad, peace be on him. The merits and the perfections which the spiritual travellers of the previous ummahs (nations) could gain, were of limited nature. After reaching the stage of passing away from self they could view the Divine Names and Attributes, but could not advance any further. The reason was that the highest stage of their gnosis was the maxim, "There is no deity, but Allah" which meant the version of Allah's most Beautiful Names and Attributes. On the other hand the spiritual travellers of the Islamic ummah have reached several higher stages which cannot be described in words. The reason is that the guiding light of all Islamic rules is the maxim, "Allah is far above being described', The spiritual progress of a Muslim devotee being connected with this maxim, the stages which he can traverse, are too high to be explained. That is why even the former Prophets could think of no station higher than that of the vision of the Divine Names and Attributes, with the result that they had to face many difficulties and hardships, and were able to get rid of them only by invoking the station of the spiritual guardianship of the Holy Prophet, Imam Ali, Fatimah Zahra and their progeny. It was the spiritual guardianship of these personalities that delivered the former Prophets from their worries and grief. Although the former Prophets were to a certain extent conscious of the high position of the Imams and that is why they invoked it, but till the end of their life they did not know all its characteristics. Some Qur'anic verses show that only Prophet Ibrahim once or twice viewed these higher truths, but only momentarily. The permanent vision of them will be in the other world only.

Before quoting the Qur'anic verses in support of our point it may be mentioned that the text of the Qur'an clearly shows that the position of sincerity also has several grades, for a number of Prophets who held this position to a certain extent, could not attain to its higher grades, for which they used to pray to Allah. For example the Qur'an says about Prophet Yusuf that: Surely he was of Our single minded slaves (Surah Yusuf, 12:24). Still he prayed to Allah saying: You are my protecting friend in this world and the Hereafter. Make me to die submissive to you and join me to the righteous (Surah Yusuf, 12:101)

The prayer shows that he did not attain the position he was praying for during his life time and so he prayed that he might be granted it after his death. Whether his prayer would be fulfilled in the hereafter, the Qur'an is silent on this point. Prophet Ibrahim held a high position in the station of sincerity, yet he prays saying: My Lord, vouchsafe me wisdom and unite me to the righteous (Surah ash-Shu'ara, 26:83)

This shows that the station of the righteous is higher than that of sincerity. That is why Prophet Ibrahim wanted to be joined to those who occupied this position. Allah did not accede to his prayer in this world, but promised to grant him the position he asked for in the hereafter: Surely We chose him in this world and he will be among the righteous in the hereafter (Surah al-Baqarah, 2:130).

It may be noted that the position of righteousness for which the former Prophets craved, is different from that which was conferred on Prophet Ibrahim and his descendants according to the following verse: We bestowed upon him Ishaq and Ya'qub as a grandson. Each of them We made righteous. (Surah al-Anbiya, 21:72)

This kind of righteousness they all enjoyed including Prophet Ibrahim himself. But he was still praying to be joined to the righteous. That shows that he wished something higher than what he had already been granted.

As for the fact that the Holy Prophet and some other persons during their lifetime occupied this higher position, is clear from the following verse:

Surely my Guardian is Allah who revealed the Book. He befriends the righteous. (Surah al-A'raf, 7:196)

According to this verse, first the Holy Prophet admits that Allah is his Guardian and then declares that his guardian is He who befriends and protects the righteous. This shows that at that time there existed certain individuals occupying the position of righteousness, whom Allah befriended. This also shows why the former Prophets made their prayers through the medium of the Imams and what a high position was held by those righteous individuals whom even great Prophets like Ibrahim wished to join.

As for the fact that the great Prophets attained to the position of sincerity, it can be inferred from a number of Qur'anic verses in different ways. The Qur'an expressly says that only the people of sincerity can eulogize Allah in a befitting manner. Allah says: Glorified be Allah from what they attributed to Him, except the single minded slaves of Allah, whose case is different (Surah as Saffat, 37:160).

Ordering the Holy Prophet to eulogize Him, Allah says: Say; Praise be to Allah and peace be on His slaves whom He has chosen. Is Allah best or all that they ascribe to Him as partners? (Surah an-Naml, 27:59).

The Qur'an cites Prophet Ibrahim praising Allah in the following words: Praise be to Allah who has given me in my old age Isma'il and Ishaq. My Lord is indeed the hearer of prayer. (Surah Ibrahim, 14:39)

Prophet Nuh was ordered to glorify Allah in the following words: Then say: Praise be to Allah who has saved us from the wrong doing people. (Surah al-Mu'minun, 23:28)

Concerning certain eminent Prophets the Qur'an expressly says that they held the position of sincerity. About Prophet Yusuf the Qur'an says: Surely he is of Our single minded slaves. (Surah Yusuf, 12:24)

About Prophet Musa it says: And make mention in the Book of Musa. He was single minded, and he was a messenger of Allah, a Prophet. (Surah Maryam, 19:51)

About Prophets Ibrahim, Ishaq and Ya'qub the Qur'an says: And make mention of Our slaves, Ibrahim, Ishaq and Ya'qub, men of parts and vision. We purified them with a pure thought, remembrance of the Home of the hereafter (Surah Sad, 38:45)

According to the following verse Satan can do no harm to the men sincerily devoted to Allah: He said: Then by Your might, I surely will beguile every one of them, save Your single-minded slaves among them. (Surah Sad, 38:82)

Only those who are not thankful to Allah are seduced by Satan: I shall come upon them from before them, and from behind them and from their right hands and from their left hands, and You will not find most of them thankful to You. (Surah al-A'raf, 7:17)

Concerning several Prophets the Qur'an says that they were chosen by Allah: We bestowed upon him Ishaq and Ya'qub, each of them We guided; and Nuh We guided before. From among his descendants We guided Dawud, Sulayman, Ayyub, Yusuf, Musa and Harun. Thus do we reward the good, And We guided Zakariyah, Yahya, Isa and Ilyas. Each one of them was righteous. And We guided Isma'il, Alyasa', Yunus and Lut. We gave each of them precedence over the rest of the people. And We guided some of their forefathers, children and brothers. We picked them and guided them to a straight path. (Surah al-An'am, 6:84-87)

From these verses it may be inferred that all the Prophets held the position of sincerity, whereas in the verses mentioned earlier only a few Prophets were mentioned. In these verses Allah has said that He 'picked them', that is He chose them from so many people.

Those who are beguiled and seduced by Satan are those who are not thankful to Allah. Therefore we can say that those who are thankful to Him cannot be entrapped by Satan for they are sincerely devoted to

Allah. Whenever the Qur'an describes anyone as thankful, we can easily conclude that he is one of Allah's single-minded and sincere slaves. For example, the Qur'an says about Prophet Nuh: They were the descendants of those whom We carried (in the ship) along with Nuh. Surely he was a thankful slave. (Surah Bani Isra'il, 17:3)

About Prophet Lut it says: We sent a storm of stones upon all of them, except the family of Lut whom We rescued in the last watch of the night as a grace from Us. Thus we reward him who is thankful (Surah al-Qamar, 54:34-35)

About Prophet Ibrahim it says: Surely Ibrahim was a nation, obedient to Allah, by nature upright and he was not one of the idolaters. He was thankful for Allah's bounties. Allah chose him and guided him to a straight path. (Surah an-Nahl, 16:120)

All the other Prophets who have been described as thankful are in principle men of sincerity.

In the above verse Allah says: We picked them from amongst all men as if they were taken up carefully and put somewhere safely. On this basis the case of those who have been picked is different from all other men. They are the people who are exclusively devoted to Allah and are especially favored by Him. This picking by Allah applies to the people of sincerity only because they have attached themselves exclusively to Him and have severed their relations from everything else. Besides, picking in this verse is not related only to those mentioned in it by name, for Allah says: "We guided some of their forefathers, children and brothers. We picked them and guided them to a straight path". Here the word brothers means moral and spiritual brothers, of these Prophets, that is those who share spiritual knowledge with them. Therefore the statement appears to be applying to all Prophets, and it may safely be argued that all Prophets are the people of sincerity.

Chapter 5

Seeking Allah's Guidance

Allamah Muhammad Husayn Tabatabai

The first thing that a spiritual traveller has to do is to inquire into various religions as far as possible so that he may become conversant with the unity and guidance of Allah. He should try to acquire at least as much knowledge as be enough for practical purposes. Having carried out this kind of investigation into the unity of Allah and the Prophethood of the Holy Prophet he will come out of the domain of infidelity and enter that of minor Islam and minor faith. This is the knowledge about which there is a unanimity of opinion among the jurists that its acquisition is essential for every obligated person for the purpose of acknowledging the fundamental beliefs on the basis of proofs and arguments. If a person cannot get the required degree of satisfaction despite his best efforts he should not lose heart and should pray for obtaining it with humility and submissiveness. This is the method that is reported to have been followed by the Prophet Idris and his followers.

The prayer with humility means that the spiritual traveller should admit his weakness, and earnestly seek guidance from Allah who always helps those who seek the truth earnestly. The Qur'an says'. Those who strive in Us We will surely guide them to our path. (Surah al-Ankabut, 29:69)

I remember when I was in Najaf receiving spiritual and moral training from Haji Mirza Ali Qazi, one morning I fell dozing while I was sitting on the prayer rug. All of a sudden I saw as if two persons were sitting in front of me. One of them was Prophet Idris and other was my brother, Muhammad Husayn Tabatabai. Prophet Idris began talking. He was speaking to me, but I was hearing what he said through the medium of my brother. He said: "During my life I faced many knotty problem which appeared to be too difficult to be resolved, but they were resolved automatically. It seemed that they were resolved by some supernatural hand from the unseen world. These events for the first time revealed to me the connection between this world and the metaphysical world, and established my relation to what is beyond this world."

I felt at that time that the problems and difficulties to which Prophet Idris was referring were the events which he experienced during his childhood. What he meant was that if anybody sought guidance from Allah earnestly, Allah would surely help him. While seeking help from Allah chanting of some appropriate verses of the Qur'an repeatedly will be very useful. Allah says: "Remember that with the remembrance of Allah the hearts are satisfied." The repeated chanting of "Ya Fattahu" "Ya dalilal Mutahayyirin" will also be found useful. Anyhow, the chanting must be with full attention and concentration.

One of my friends relates that once he was going by bus from Iran to Karbala. A sturdy young man was sitting near him. No conversation had taken place between them. Then all of a sudden the young man began to cry. My friend was astonished. He asked the young man what was the matter. He said: "I will certainly tell you my story. I am a civil engineer. Since my childhood I was so brought up that I became an atheist. I did not believe in resurrection, but I had a feeling of love for the religious people, whether they were Muslims, Christians or Jews. One night I was attending a party of my friends where some Bahais1 were also present. For some time we all took part in games, music and dance, but soon I began to feel ashamed of myself and so I went upstairs and began to weep. I said: O' God! Help me if you really do exist! After a few moments I came downstairs. At dawn we all dispersed. In the evening while I was going on some professional duty along with my team in-charge and some officers, I suddenly saw a religious scholar with an illuminated face coming towards me. He greeted me and said that he wanted to have some talk with me. I told him that I would see him next day in the afternoon. After he had left some people objected to my giving a cold reception to quite a well known holy man. I said that I thought he was some needy person, who wanted my help. By chance it so happened that my team in-charge asked me to be present next day in the afternoon at a particular place and do a certain job. The time which he gave me was exactly which I had given to that religious scholar. I said to myself that there was no more any possibility of going to him. Next day at the appointed time I felt that I was not feeling well. In a few moments I had a high fever and it became necessary to call a doctor. Naturally I was unable to go for the job entrusted to me by my in-charge. But as soon as the representative of the in-charge went away, I felt myself relieved. My temperature had become normal. I thought over my condition and was convinced that the incident had some secret. Therefore I got up immediately and went to that scholar's place. When I saw him, he began to talk of fundamental principles and proved each one of them to my entire satisfaction. Then he asked me to come to him next day again. For several days I went to him daily. Each day when I visited him he told me so many things in detail about my private affairs about which nobody other than me alone knew at all. A lot of time passed in this way. One day my friends pressed me to attend one of their parties. There I had to take part in gambling also. Next day when I called on that scholar he at once said: "Don't you feel ashamed? How come that you committed such a grave sin?" Tears flowed down from my eyes. I admitted my mistake and said that I was sorry. He said: "Have a bath for repentance, and don't do such a thing again". Then he gave me some other instructions. Thus he changed the program of my life. All this happened in Zanjan. Later when I was going to Tehran he asked me to call upon certain scholars there. At last he asked me to go on a pilgrimage to the holy places. Now I am going on the journey which he asked me to undertake."

My friend said: "When we approached Iraq. I saw that young man weeping again. On my inquiry he said: "It appears that we have entered the land of Iraq, for Abu Abdillah (Imam Husayn) has welcomed me."

This story has been narrated to show that anybody seeking guidance from Allah earnestly is bound to succeed in his objective. Even if he is skeptical about Monotheism - the unity of Allah, he will receive guidance.

Having successfully completed this stage the spiritual traveller should strive for attaining to major Islam and major faith. In this connection the first thing to do is to know the rules of Islamic law. This knowledge should be acquired from some competent jurist. Next to acquiring the knowledge of law comes the turn of practicing it. It is very necessary to always act according to Islamic law, for knowledge is the best incentive to action, and action produces conviction. If a person is certain about the veracity of his knowledge, he is bound to act according to it. If he does not, that means that he is not convinced of the correctness of what he knows, and that his knowledge and belief are no more than a sort of mental impression. For example, if somebody is sure of Allah's absolute providence, he will never desperately try to earn money at all costs. He will be satisfied with what the Islamic injunctions allow him and will try to earn with tranquil happiness what is necessary for him and his family. But if a man is always worried about his livelihood, that means that he does not believe in the absolute providence of Allah or thinks that it is conditional on his trying hard, or he believes that providence is limited to earning cash or salary. That is what is meant when it is said that knowledge is an incentive to action. The following similitude shows how action enhances knowledge. When a person says from the core of his heart: "Glory and praise be to my exalted Lord", he acknowledges his helplessness and humbleness. Naturally, power and glory cannot be conceived without there being a conception of humbleness and helplessness. Conversely no one can be powerless without there being a powerful. Therefore the mind of the person saying: "Glory and praise be to my exalted Lord" while prostrating himself in prayers, is naturally diverted to the absolute power and glory of Allah.2 This is what is meant by saying that action promotes knowledge. The Qur'anic verse, The good deed He promotes it (Surah al-Fatir, 35:10) also refers to this fact.

It is necessary for the spiritual traveller to do his best to abide by all that is obligatory and to refrain from all that is forbidden, for doing anything against Islamic injunctions is absolutely contrary to the spirit of his spiritual journey. It is no use to perform commendable deeds and spiritual exercises if the heart and soul are polluted, just as it serves no useful purpose to apply cosmetics if the body is dirty. Besides being very particular about performing what is obligatory and abstaining from what is forbidden, it is also imperative for the spiritual traveller to take interest in performing commendable deeds and avoiding obnoxious ones, for attaining to major Islam and major faith depends on doing that. It is to be remembered that every deed has a corresponding effect and contributes to the completion of faith. The following tradition reported by Muhammad bin Muslim refers to this point: "Faith depends on the deeds for the deeds are essential part of faith. Faith cannot be firmly established without good deeds."

Therefore the spiritual traveller must perform every commendable act at least once so that he may attain that part of faith also which depends on the performance of that particular act. Imam Ali has said that it is deeds that produce perfect faith. Hence it is necessary for the spiritual traveller not to overlook commendable deeds while advancing towards the stage of major faith, for his faith will be incomplete in proportion to his lack of interest in the performance of good deeds. If a devotee purified his tongue and his other organs but at the time of spending money was negligent of his duty, his faith would not be perfect. Every bodily organ must get that part of faith which is related to it. The heart which is the chief of all organs should be kept busy with remembering the Names and Attributes of Allah and pondering over the Divine signs in men and the universe. That is the way how man's heart imbibes the spirit of faith. The Qur'an says: It may be noted that with the remembrance of Allah the hearts become satisfied. (Surah ar-Ra'd, 13:28)

When every organ has obtained its due share of faith, the devotee should intensify his spiritual effort and enter the domain of certainty and conviction by completing the stages of major Islam and major faith.

Those who believe and obscure not their belief by wrong doing, theirs is safety; and they are rightly guided. (Surah al-An'am, 6:82)

As a result of doing spiritual exercises the spiritual traveller will not only be placed on the right path, but will also become safe from the assaults of Satan.

Remember that no fear shall come upon the friends of Allah, nor shall they grieve. (Surah Hud, 10:62)

Fear means apprehension of impending danger or evil that causes worry and alarm. Grief means mental distress and sorrow caused by the occurrence of something evil and unpleasant. The spiritual traveller has no apprehension nor sorrow, for he entrusts all his affairs to Allah. He has no objective other than Allah. Such people as they enter the domain of certainty have been described by Allah as His friends. Imam Ali hinted at this stage when he said: "He sees Allah's path, walks on His way, knows His signs and crosses the obstacles. He is at such a stage of certainty that it seems as if he was seeing everything by the light of the sun".

Imam Ali has also said: "Knowledge has given them real insight; they have imbibed the spirit of conviction; they consider easy what the people living in ease and luxury consider difficult; they are familiar with what the ignorant have aversion to; their bodies are in the world but their souls are in high heaven."

At this stage the doors of vision and inspiration are opened before the spiritual traveller.

Evidently there is no inconsistency between passing through these stages and the spiritual traveller's being busy with his basic necessities in the world. His inner experience has nothing to do with his external activities such as his marriage, earning his livelihood and being engaged in trade or cultivation. The spiritual traveller lives bodily in this mundane world and takes part in worldly activities, but his soul goes round the angelic world and talks with its inmates. He is like a bereaved person whose some close relative has died recently. Such a person lives among the people, talks to them, walks to various places, eats and sleeps, but his heart is always lamenting over the memory of his relative. Whoever looked at him, could understand that he was in a wretched state of mind.

Similarly a spiritual traveller despite his being engaged in fulfilling his natural needs, maintains his contact with Allah. A fire of love is always burning in his heart. The pain of separation keeps him restless, but no one except Allah knows his inner condition, though the onlookers also can in general discern that love for Allah and for truth has befallen him. It is clear from this explanation that the wailing, weeping and prayer of the Imams were not fake, nor were the supplications which have come down from them purely for instructional purposes. Such a notion is based on the ignorance of facts. It is below the dignity of the Imams to say anything unrealistic or to call people to Allah by means of fake prayers. Will it be proper to say that the heart-rending wailings of Imam Ali and Imam Zaynul 'Abidin were fake and had no reality or they were for teaching purpose only? Not at all. This group of the leaders of religion have attained to the stage of passing away from self and abiding in Allah after completing all the stages of spiritual journey and hence combine in themselves the qualities relating to the world of unity as well as the world of plurality. They receive Divine light in every walk of life and are required to maintain their attention to the higher world and not to violate any rule relating to that world even slightly.

When the spiritual traveller has traversed all the above mentioned worlds successfully and overcome Satan, he enters the world of victory and conquest. At that time he will have passed the material world and entered the world of souls. Hence forward his great journey will be through the angelic world and the spiritual world and ultimately he will succeed in reaching the world of Divinity.

Notes:

1. A hundred year old religious community like Qadyanis.

2. The supplications which have come down to us from the Holy Prophet and his Household provide the best means of our moral and spiritual training. They strengthen faith; create a spirit of self- sacrifice and promote a taste for performing acts of worship and praying to Allah. The Supplication of Mujir, the Supplication of Kumayl, the Supplication of Abu Hamzah Thumali and the Supplication of 'Arafah may be mentioned in this connection.

Chapter 6

Rules of Attaining Spiritual Perfection

Allamah Muhammad Husayn Tabatabai

To be able to advance on this spiritual path it is necessary for a spiritual traveler to appoint some righteous man his preceptor (spiritual guide). The preceptor must have passed away from self and reached the station of ever lasting abode in Allah. He should be fully aware of all the points which are to the advantage or disadvantage of a spiritual traveler and should be capable of undertaking the training and guidance of other spiritual travelers. Moreover, remembrance and recollection of Allah and prayer to Him with humility are also necessary for a spiritual traveler. Besides, to be able to pass all the stages of spiritual path successfully it is necessary for him to observe certain rules:

(i) Renunciation of customs, usages and social formalities
It means to refrain from all those formalities which are related to mere customs or stylish living and which are a hindrance in the way of the spiritual traveler, who is required to live among the people but to lead a simple and balanced life. Some people are so absorbed in social formalities that they always observe them too minutely in order to maintain their position in society and often indulge in useless and even harmful practices, which cause nothing but inconvenience and worry. They give preference to unnecessary usages over the real and important necessities. Their criterion for judging what is proper and what is improper is the appreciation and disapproval of the common people. They do not have any opinion of their own, and simply follow the common trend. At the other end there are some other people who lead an isolated life and ignore all rules of society and thus deprive themselves from all social benefits. They do not mix with other people and come to be known as cynics. To be successful in his objective the spiritual traveler should follow the middle way. He should mix up with the people neither too much nor too

little. It does not matter if he looked different from other people because of his distinct social behaviour. He should not follow others and should not care for any criticism in this connection. Allah says: They do not fear the criticism of any critic in the way of Allah. (Surah al-Ma'ida, 5:54). That means that the true believer sticks to what he thinks to be right. As a principle it may be said that the spiritual traveler should weigh every matter seriously and should not follow the wishes of other people or their opinion blindly.

(ii) Determination

As soon as the spiritual traveler begins his spiritual exercises, he is bound to face many unpleasant events. He is criticized by his friends and acquaintances who are interested only in their selfish desires and current social customs. They taunt and unbraid the spiritual traveler in order to bring a change in his behaviour and to turn him away from his objective. When these worldly people find that the spiritual traveler has a new style of life and his ways and manners have become different from their own, they feel upset and try their best to remove him by means of mockery and taunt from the line recently chosen by him. Thus at every stage of his spiritual journey the devotee has to face fresh difficulties which he can resolve only by means of his determination, perseverance, will power and trust in Allah. Let the believers place their trust in Allah. (Surah Ali Imran, 3:122)

(iii) Moderation

It is one of those important principles which the spiritual traveler must follow, for a little negligence in this respect not only hampers his progress, but often as a consequence of a lack of attention to this principle he may get tired of the spiritual journey itself. In the beginning the spiritual traveler may show much zeal and fervor. In the middle he may see wonderful manifestations of Divine light, and consequently may decide to spend most of his time in acts of worship and make himself busy with prayer, bewailing and weeping. Thus he may try to undertake everything good and pick up a morsel of every spiritual dish. But this practice is not only not beneficial but is also in many cases definitely harmful. Under too much pressure he may get fed up, leave the work incomplete and cease to take interest in commendable acts. Too much enthusiasm in the beginning leads to too little interest in the end. Therefore the spiritual traveler should not be misled by momentary zeal, and keeping in view his personal circumstances should shoulder only as much burden, or even less, as he is sure to be able to carry permanently maintaining due interest in it. He should perform acts of worship when he is really inclined to them and should withdraw from them when his desire to perform them has not still completely faded away. He may be compared to a man who wants to eat something. Such a man first of all should choose a dish that agrees to his temperament, and then should stop eating it before his belly is full. This principle of moderation is derived from that tradition also according to which Imam Ja'far Sadiq said to Abdul Aziz Qaratisi: "Abdul Aziz, faith has ten degrees like the steps of a ladder which are climbed one by one. If you find anyone below you by one step, pull him up to you gently and do not burden him with what he cannot bear, or else you will break him."

This tradition shows that in principle only those acts of worship are beneficial which are performed with zeal and eagerness. The following saying of Imam Sadiq also means the same thing: "Do not force yourselves to worship."

(iv) Steadiness

It means that after feeling penitence about a sin and asking Allah's forgiveness for it, it must not be committed again. Every vow must be fulfilled and every promise made to the pious preceptor must be kept.

(v) Continuance

Before explaining this point it is necessary to make some preliminary remarks. The Qur'anic verses and religious reports show that everything we perceive by our senses, everything we do and everything that exists or occurs has a corresponding truth transcending this material and physical world and not subject to any limitations of time and space. When these truths descend to this material world, they assume a tangible and palpable form. The Qur'an expressly says: There is not a thing the treasures of which we do not have with Us. But we send down everything in an appointed measure. (Surah al-Hijr, 15:21)

This verse essentially means that everything in this world has had an existence free from estimation and measurement prior to its material existence. When Allah intends to send a thing to this world, He appoints its measure and so it becomes limited: No disaster befalls in the earth or in yourselves, but it is in a Book before We bring it into being. Surely this is easy for Allah. (Surah al-Hadid, 57:22)

As the external shape of everything is fixed and limited and everything is subject to all the changes that are the characteristics of matter such as coming into a shape and being disfigured, everything in this world is temporary, transient and subject to decay. Allah says: Whatever is with you is to be exhausted and whatever is with Allah is to stay. (Surah an-Nahl, 16:96) In other words, those abstract truths which are not subject to material characteristics and the treasures of which are with Allah, are not to come to an end. The following tradition, which is accepted by the Shi'ah and the Sunnis both, is also relevant in this connection: "We, the Prophets have been ordered to speak to the people according to their intellectual capacity."

This tradition relates to the description of the truths, not to their quantity. It says that the Prophets simplify the higher truths and describe them in a way comprehensible to their addresses. Human mind having been dazzled by the glamour of the world and being preoccupied with the futile desires, has become dull and rusty and is not capable of comprehending the reality of the truths. The Prophets may be compared to a man who wants to explain some truth to the children. Naturally he will have to explain it in a way corresponding to the power of understanding and observation of the children. The same rule applies to the Prophets who are the custodians of the Divine teachings. Sometimes they describe the living truths in such a way that they appear to be lifeless, while as a matter of fact even the external rites such as prayers, fast, pilgrimage, zakat, khums, urging that what is right and restraining from that what is evil are all living and conscious truths.

The spiritual traveler is he who by means of a spiritual journey and spiritual exercises seeks to purify his soul and intellect from all impurities to be able to view the higher truths by the grace of Allah in this very life and this very world. It often happens that a devotee views the ablution and prayers in their real form and feels that from the viewpoint of perception and consciousness, their real form is a thousand times better than their physical form.

The reports which have come down to us from the Imams show that the acts of worship will appear on the Day of Resurrection in their appropriate forms and will talk to the human beings. Even in the Qur'an it has been mentioned that the ears, the eyes and other organs will be speaking on that day. Similarly the mosques which appear to be composed of bricks and mortar, have a living and conscious reality. That is why some reports say that on the Day of Judgement the mosques and the Holy Qur'an will make complaints to their Lord. One day a gnostic was lying on his bed. When he turned from one side to the other he heard a shriek coming out of the ground. He could not immediately know the reason.

Subsequently either he himself realized or somebody else pointed out to him that the ground, having been separated from him, was shrieking.

After these preliminary remarks now we come to our main point. By means of continuous practice the spiritual traveler should imprint on his mind an abstract figure of each act of worship he performs, so that his practice of it may turn into a permanent habit. He should perform each deed again and again and should not give it up till he begins to take delight in its performance. He cannot capture the permanent angelic aspect of a deed unless he continues to perform for quite a long time so that its impression on his mind may become indelible. For this purpose he should choose a deed consistent with his inclination and aptitude and then continue to perform it, for if a deed was abandoned prematurely, not only its good effects would be obliterated, but a reaction also would begin to appear. As a good deed is luminous, the reaction of its abandonment involves darkness and evil. The fact is that "there is nothing but good with Allah and all the evils, mischief and wrongs are attributable to us." Therefore man is responsible for all faults and defects. "My Lord, evil cannot be attributed to You." This shows that Allah's favor is common to all. It is not a prerogative of any particular class. Allah's infinite mercy is for all human beings, whether Muslims, Jews, Christians, Zoroastrians or idol-worshippers. But some men because of their wrong doing develop certain characteristics which make them unhappy, and so Allah's mercy makes some people happy and some others distressed.

(vi) Meditation

This means that the spiritual traveler must at no time be forgetful of his duty and must always abide by the decision which he has taken.

Meditation or contemplation is very vast in its meaning and its sense differs according to the degrees and stages of the spiritual journey. In the beginning it means refraining from all acts not useful in this world or the hereafter and abstaining from saying or doing anything disliked by Allah. Gradually this meditation becomes stiffer and higher, and may sometimes mean concentration on one's silence, or on one's self or on a higher truth, that is the names and the attributes of Allah. The degrees and grades of this kind of meditation will be mentioned later.

Here it may be mentioned that meditation is an important factor in spiritual journey. The leading gnostics have laid great stress on it, and have described it as the foundation stone of spiritual journey on which the edifice of remembrance and recollection of Allah rests. Without meditation remembrance and recollection of Allah are not likely to produce any positive results. For a spiritual traveler meditation is as important as for a patient the prescribed course of diet, without which the medicines may be ineffective or may even produce counter-effects. That is why the most outstanding spiritual guides do not allow any liturgies and recollection of Allah without meditation.

(vii) Checking
It means that the spiritual traveler should every day have a fixed time for checking and assessing what he had done during the past 24 hours. The idea of this checking has been derived from what Imam Musa ibn Ja'far has said: "He who does not take account of himself once every day is not one of us." If on checking the spiritual traveler finds that he has not done his duty, he should seek forgiveness from Allah and if he finds that he has performed his duty in every respect, he should be thankful to Him.

(viii) Censuring
If the spiritual traveler finds that he is guilty of some lapse or error, he should take some suitable action to reprimand or punish himself.

(ix) Hastening
This means that the spiritual traveler should be quick in implementing the decision he has taken. As he is likely to face many obstacles on his way, he should be vigilant and careful and should try to achieve his objective without wasting a moment.

(x) Faith and Reliance
The spiritual traveler must have love for and implicit faith in the Holy Prophet and his rightful successors.[1] Complete reliance and trust are especially necessary at this stage. The more the reliance, the more lasting the effect of good deeds.
As all the existing things are the creation of Allah, the spiritual traveler must love all of them and should have regard for them according to the grade of their dignity. A lover of Allah shows kindness to all men and animals. According to a tradition, affection for the creation is a part of faith in Allah.
Another tradition says: "Allah, I seek of You Your love and the love of him who loves You."

(xi) Observance of the Rules of Veneration
The observance of these rules of correct behaviour towards all and His

vicegerents is different from the faith and reliance mentioned above. Here veneration means to be careful not to exceed one's limits and do anything inconsistent with the requirements of man's servitude to Allah. It is essential for man to observe his limits vis-a-vis his Creator, the essentially existing Being. This veneration is a requirement of this world of plurality, whereas faith and love naturally require attention to monotheism - the unity of Allah.

Faith and veneration stand in the same relationship to each other as an act obligatory and an act prohibited. While performing an obligatory act the devotee looks towards Allah and while abstaining from a prohibited act he looks towards his own limitations lest he should exceed them. Veneration means following a middle way between fear and hope. Not to observe the rules of veneration indicates too much familiarity which is extremely undesirable.

The distinctive characteristic of the late Haji Mirza Ali Agha Qazi was his cheerfulness and faith rather than fear. The same was true of the late Haji Shaykh Muhammad Bahar. On the contrary, the predominant feature of Haji Mirza Jawid Agha Maliki was fear rather than hope and cheerfulness. That is what is indicated by their sayings. According to the gnostic parlance he who is dominated by cheerfulness is called a "drunkard" and he who is dominated by fear is called a "hymist". The best thing is to adopt a middle way in between these two extremes. In other words the devotee should have the highest degree of both the qualities at one and the same time. This degree of excellence is found in the case of the Imams only.

In short, man who is a possibly existing being, should not forget his limits. That is why Imam Ja'far Sadiq used to prostrate himself on the ground whenever anything smacking extremism was uttered by anybody about him.

An absolutely dutiful devotee is he who always considers himself to be present before Allah and observes all the rules of property and deference while doing anything such as talking, keeping quiet, eating, drinking, sleeping etc. If the devotee kept the names and attributes of Allah in his mind, he would automatically observe all the rules of veneration and would always be conscious of his humility.

(xii) Intention

It means that the spiritual traveler should be single minded and well-intentioned. The objective of his spiritual journey should be nothing but to pass away in Allah. The Qur'an says: "Worship Allah keeping worship purely for Him."

A number of reports say that there are three grades of intention. Imam Sadiq is reported to have said: "There are three kinds of worshippers: There are some who worship Allah because they are afraid of Him. Their worship is that of the slaves. There are some others who worship Allah for the sake of recompense. Their worship is that of the wage-earners. There are till others who worship Allah because they love Him. Their worship is that of freemen."

On deep thinking it appears that there are two kinds of worship. One of them is not worship at all in the right sense, because those who perform this kind of worship are actually self-worshippers. They are motivated by self-interest. As self-worshippers cannot be the worshippers of Allah, they may even be regarded as a sort of unbelievers.

The Qur'an has described the worship of Allah as man's nature. At the same time it has denied the possibility of any change in man's in-born qualities.

Set your purpose for religion as a man by nature upright - the nature in which Allah has created man. There is no altering in the nature framed by Allah. That is the right religion, but most men do not know 'even this fact' (Surah ar-Rum, 30:30)

Therefore an act of worship actuated by self-interest is not only a deviation from the path of devotion to Allah, but is also a deviation from the path of monotheism, for these self-seekers appear not to believe in the unity of Allah in His actions and attributes because they associate someone else with Him. The Qur'an has everywhere proclaimed the unity of Allah and has denied the existence of any associate or partner with Him. The first two groups of worshippers mentioned above consider Allah to be their partner in their objectives and do not refrain from the idea of self-aggrandizement even in worshipping Him. They have double objective and that is what is called polytheism which according to the Qur'an is an unforgivable offence.

Allah does not forgive that partners should be ascribed to Him. He pardons all save that to whom He will (Surah an-Nisa', 4:48, 116)

It is clear from the above that the worship performed by the first two groups is not fruitful and will not bring the worshipper closer to Allah.

As for the third group who worships Allah for the sake of love, their worship is that of freemen, and according to a report the most noble worship. "It is a hidden position to which only the pure attain." Love means attraction, or in other words to be drawn by some person or some truth.

The third group is of those who love Allah and are inclined towards Him. They have no objective other than being drawn to Him and gain His good pleasure. Their motive is their Real Beloved and they try to move towards Him.

Some reports say that Allah should be worshipped because He deserves being worshipped. He is fit and worthy of being worshipped because of His attributes. In other words He is to be worshipped because He is Allah.

Imam Ali says: "My Lord, I do not worship You because I am afraid of Your hell, nor because I want Your paradise. I worship You because I have found You fit for being worshipped. You Yourself have guided me to You and have called me to You. Had You not been I would not have known what You are."

In the beginning the spiritual traveler goes forward with the help of love, but after traversing a few stages he realizes that love is different from the beloved. Therefore he tries to give up love which was his means of progress so far, but which might prove a hindrance in his further advancement. Now he concentrates all his attention on the Beloved Whom he worships as his Beloved only. When he goes a few steps further he realizes that yet his worship is not free from duality for he still considers himself to be the lover and Allah the beloved, while it is inconsistent with absolute unity of Allah to think of a lover of Him. Therefore the spiritual traveler tries to forget about love so that he may step into the world of unity from the world of plurality. At this stage he ceases to have will and intention for his distinctive personality has already passed away.

Prior to this stage the spiritual traveler was seeking vision, viewing and sight. Now he forgets all these things, for when he has no intention, he can have no desire. In this state it cannot be said whether the eyes and the heart of the spiritual traveler are functioning or not. To see and not to see, to know and not to know all become irrelevant.

Bayazid Bistami is reported to have said: "First I renounced the world. Next day I renounced the hereafter. The third day I renounced everything other than Allah. The fourth day I was asked what I wanted. I said: I want that I do not want." Perhaps taking a clue from this saying some people have fixed the following four stages:

(i) Renunciation of this world; (ii) Renunciation of the hereafter; (iii) Renunciation of the Lord; (iv) Renunciation of renunciation. This is a point which requires deep consideration for being understood properly. This is the stage at which the spiritual traveler gives up all desires. This is, a great achievement, but difficult to realize, for even at this stage the spiritual traveler finds that his heart is not free from all desires and intentions. At least he aspires to gain perfection. It is of no use to make any conscious effort to get rid of the desires for such an effort itself involves a desire and an objective.

One day I spoke to my teacher, Mirza Ali Agha Qazi about this question and asked him what the solution of this problem was. He said that it could be resolved by adopting the method of "burning". The spiritual traveler should realize that Allah has created him in such a way that he must always have some desires and ambitions. That is a part of his inborn nature. Howsoever he may try, he cannot eliminate all desires. Therefore he should realize his powerlessness and give up all efforts to that effect. In that case he will entrust his case to Allah. The feeling of powerlessness will not only purify him, but will also burn the roots of all desire. Anyhow, it must be kept in mind that only theoretical knowledge of this point is not enough. The spiritual traveler must develop a real taste for it. If such a taste is developed, it can be more pleasure-giving than anything else in the world.

This method is called 'burning' for it burns out the very existence of will and intention and uproots them completely.

The Qur'an has used this method on a number of occasions. One instance is the use of the Divine expression: "We belong to Allah and to Him we shall return." Anybody who uses this method will find that it produces very quick results.

At the time of calamities, disasters and mishaps man consoles himself in different ways. For example, he reminds himself that death and misfortunes are the destiny of all human beings. But Allah has suggested the burning method as a short cut by prescribing the above formula to be uttered on such occasions. If man realizes that he himself and all that he possesses and all that belongs to him in any way, are all owned by Allah who has full power and authority to dispose of them as He wills and pleases, he will not grieve for any loss and will feel relieved. Man should know that factually he is not the owner of anything. His ownership is only phenomenal. In reality everything belongs to Allah who gives whatever He will and takes away whatever He will. Nobody has a right to interfere in what He does. Man should know that he has been created wishful, ambitious and needy. All that is a part of his inborn nature. Therefore, when the spiritual traveler is filled with any sort of yearning during his spiritual journey, he suspects that it is not possible for him to be totally free from desires, and that passing away in Allah, which is the basis of the worship of freemen, is inconsistent with his inmate propensities to will and desire. In these circumstances he is perplexed and feels helpless. But it is this feeling of helplessness that effaces his egoism, which is the basis of will and desire. Therefore, after passing this stage no trace of will and desire is left. This point is worth understanding well.

(xiii) Silence

There are two kinds of silence: (i) general and relative; (ii) particular and absolute. Relative silence means to refrain from talking to people in excess to what is absolutely required. This kind of silence is necessary for the spiritual traveler at every stage. It is commendable for others also. Imam Ja'far Sadiq referred to this kind of silence when he said: "Our partisans (Shi'ah) are dumb." A report is mentioned in the Misbahush Shari'ah according to which Imam Ja'far Sadiq has said: "Silence is the way of the lovers of Allah because Allah likes it. It is the style of the Prophets and the habit of the chosen people."

According to another report Imam Ja'far Sidiq said:

"Silence is a part of wisdom. It is a sign of every virtue."

Particular and absolute silence means to refrain from talking during verbal recollection of Allah.

(xiv) Abstaining from Food or at least Observing Frugality

It is recommended on the condition that it should not disturb mental peace and composure. Imam Ja'far Sadiq has said: "The believer enjoys hunger. For him hunger is the food of the heart and the soul."

Hunger illuminates the soul and makes it lighter whereas overeating makes it dull and tired and hampers its soaring to the heaven of gnosis. Out of the acts of worship fasting has been lauded a great deal. A number of reports concerning the Holy Prophet's Ascension to the Heavens have been mentioned in Daylami's Irshad and the Biharul Anwar, vol. II. In these reports the Holy Prophet has been addressed as Ahmad. These reports underline the beneficial points of starvation, especially its wonderful effect in connection with spiritual journey. My teacher, the late Ali Agha Qazi once related a wonderful story about starvation. In short he said: "Once during the days of the former Prophets three persons were travelling together. At nightfall they set out in three different directions with a view to get food, but agreed to assemble next morning at a particular place at an appointed time. One of them was already invited by some person. The second man also by chance became the guest of someone. The third man had no place to go to. He said to himself that he should go to the mosque to be the guest of Allah. He passed the night in the mosque, but could get no food. Next morning they assembled at the appointed place and each one of them related his story. At that time the Prophet of the time received a revelation to the following effect: "Tell Our guest that We were his host last night and wanted to provide him with sumptuous food, but found that there was no food better than hunger."

(xv) Solitude

There are two kinds of solitude also: general and particular. General solitude means not to mix with other people especially the ignorant masses and to meet them only as and when absolutely necessary. The Qur'an says: And forsake those who rake their religion for a pastime and a jest, and whom the life of the world beguiles. (Surah al-An'am, 6:70)
Particular solitude means to keep away from all men. Such kind of seclusion is commendable at the time of performing all acts of worship, but is considered essential by the gnostics at the time of pronouncing certain liturgies. In this connection the following points must be observed:
For the spiritual traveler it is necessary to keep himself away from crowds and disturbing noises. The place where he performs acts of worship must be clean and lawful. Even the walls and the ceilings of his room must be tidy. His room should be a small one preferably accommodating only one person. A small room having no furniture and no decorating material is helpful in keeping the thoughts concentrated.
A man sought Salman Farsi's permission to build a house for him. Till then Salman had not built a house for himself. Still he refused to give the permission. That man said: "I know why you do not give permission." "Say why", said Salman. He said: "You want me to build you a house only so long and so wide that it may accommodate you only." "Yes, that's the thing. You are right", said Salman. Subsequently that man built for Salman, with his permission, a house of that small size.

(xvi) Vigil

It means that the spiritual traveler must make it a habit to wake up before dawn as early as he tolerably can. Denouncing the sleeping at dawn and praising the keeping awake at that time Allah says: They used to sleep only a little while at night and at dawn used to seek forgiveness. (Surah al-Dhariyat, 51:18)

(xvii) Continued Cleanliness

It means to be always ritually pure and to adhere to the performance of major ablution on Fridays and on all other occasions on which it has been recommended.

(xviii) Practicing modesty and humility to the utmost degree. It includes weeping and wailing also.

(xix) Abstaining from Tasty Food

The spiritual traveler should abstain from tasty dishes and should be content with a little food as is absolutely necessary to sustain his life and energy.

(xx) Secrecy

It is one of the most important points to be observed by a spiritual traveler. The great gnostics have been very particular about it and have laid great stress on it. They advised their pupils to keep their spiritual exercises as well as their visions etc. secret. If simulation (taqiyya) is not possible, equivocation (tawriyah) must be resorted to. If necessary spiritual exercises may he abandoned for some time to maintain secrecy. "Try to fulfil your needs by maintaining secrecy."

At the time of sufferings and calamities simulation and secrecy make the things easier. If the spiritual traveler faces any hardships, he should go forward patiently.

Seek help in patience and prayers; truly it is hard except for the humble-minded. (Surah al-Baqarah, 2:45)

In this verse the word salat (prayers) has been used in its literal sense, that is attention to Allah. On this basis it may be inferred from this verse that patience in the remembrance of Allah makes the hardships less burdensome and paves the way to success. That is why it is often observed that the people who become extremely restless when their small finger is cut, do not worry in the least about losing their limbs and organs in the battlefield. According to this general rule the Imams have laid great stress on secrecy, and even have considered abandoning simulation a grave sin.

Shaykh Saduq in his book, at-Tawhid has quoted a report saying that one day Abu Basir asked Imam Ja'far Sadiq if it was possible to see Allah on the Day of Resurrection. He asked so because the Asha'irah, the followers of the Sunni Imam Abul Hasan Ash'ari believe that all people will see Allah on the Day of Resurrection and in the hereafter, which is obviously not possible without incarnation. Allah is far above what these wrong-doers say. The Imam said: "It is possible to see Allah even in this world as you saw Him here just now." Abu Basir said: "Son of the Prophet, allow me to relate this event to others." The Imam did not allow him to do so and said: "Don't relate it to others; otherwise they will not be able to comprehend the truth and will go astray for no reason."

(xxi) Preceptor and Spiritual Guide
The preceptors are also of two types: General and special. The general preceptor is he who is not responsible for guiding any particular individual. People seek his guidance considering him to be a learned and experienced man. The Qur'an says: Ask those who know if you do not know. Such preceptors can be helpful only in the beginning of spiritual journey. When the spiritual traveler begins to view the manifestations of the glory of essence and attributes of Allah, he no longer needs to have a general preceptor. The special preceptor is he about whom a divine ordinance exists to the effect that he has been assigned the job of guidance. This position is held only by the Holy Prophet and his rightful successors. Their guidance and company are essential and indispensable not only at every stage of spiritual journey, but even after the spiritual traveler has reached his destination. The nature of this company is esoteric not physical for the real nature of the Imam is that station of his luminosity, the authority of which extends to everyone and everything in the world. Although Imams body is also superior to the body of everyone else, yet the source of his authority over the universe is not his body. To explain this point it may be mentioned that whatever happens in this world, its source is the names and attributes of Allah, and the same Divine names and attributes are the essence of the Imam also. That is why the Imams have said: "Allah is known through us and he is worshipped through us." Therefore, it may rightly be said that whatever stages the spiritual traveler traverses, he covers them in the light of the Imam, and every position to which he advances, that position is controlled by the Imam. Throughout his journey the spiritual traveler enjoys the company of the Imam and remains associated with him. Even after reaching his destination, he needs the company of the Imam, for it is the Imam who teaches him the rules that are to be observed in the World of Divinity. Therefore, Imam's company is essential at every stage of spiritual journey. In this connection there are many subtle points which are not easy to be explained. They may be discovered by the spiritual traveler through his own taste.

Once Muhyuddin Ibn 'Arabi went to a spiritual guide and complained to him that injustice was growing and the sins were rampant. The spiritual guide advised him to pay attention to Allah. A few days later he went to another spiritual guide and made the same complaint. That spiritual guide told him to pay attention to himself. Ibn 'Arabi was very much upset and began to weep. He asked the spiritual guide why the two answers were so different from each other. The spiritual guide said: "Oh dear! the answer is one and the same. He drew your attention to the companion and I to the path."

I have related this story to show that there is no difference between making a journey to Allah on the one hand and arriving at the station of the Imam while passing through the stages of the Divine names and attributes on the other. These two things are not only closer to each other but are almost identical. At this stage there is no conception of duality. There is nothing but the light of the glory of one Single Being, which is described in different words. Sometimes it is expressed as the Divine names and attributes and sometimes as the essence of the Imam or his luminosity.

To know whether a general preceptor is fit to be so, it is necessary to watch him closely and have contact with him for a considerable time. Such super-natural things as to know what others think, to walk on fire or water, to narrate the past events or to foretell the future, are not a sign of anybody's being a favorite of Allah. The performance of such things becomes possible at the beginning of spiritual vision, but the stage of proximity to Allah is far away from this stage. No one can be a preceptor in the true sense unless and until he receives the light of the glory of Divine essence. To receive the light of the manifestations of Divine names and attributes is not enough.

The spiritual traveler is said to be receiving the light of the manifestations of the Divine attributes when he feels that his knowledge, power and life are really the knowledge, power and life of Allah. At this stage when the spiritual traveler hears something, he feels that Allah has heard it and when he sees something, he feels that Allah has seen it. He may feel that Allah alone is the Knower, and the knowledge of every existing being is the knowledge of Allah Himself.

The spiritual traveler is said to be receiving the light of the glory of the Divine names when he views the Divine attributes in himself. For example he feels that Allah is the only Knower and his knowledge is also that of Allah. Or he feels that the only living Being is Allah and that he himself is not living, but his life is actually that of Allah. In other words he intuitively feels that "there is no knowing, living or powerful being except Allah." If a spiritual traveler receives the light of the manifestations of one or two Divine names, it is not necessary that he should receive the light of the manifestations of other Divine names also.

The spiritual traveler receives the light of the glory of Divine essence only when he forgets himself totally and can find no trace of himself or his ego. "There is none but Allah." Such a person can never go astray, nor can be seduced by Satan. Satan does not lose hope of alluring a spiritual traveler until he obliterates his very existence. But when he enters the sanctuary of the world of divinity after annihilating his personality and ego, Satan loses all hope of seducing him. A general preceptor must be such as to have reached this stage. Otherwise it is not safe for a devotee to submit himself to any Tom, Dick or Harry.

It is not advisable for a spiritual traveler to go at random to any shop for getting what he requires or to submit himself to any pretender. He should make complete investigations about the proposed preceptor and when it is not possible to do so, he should put trust in Allah, compare the proposed preceptor's teachings with those of the Holy Prophet and the Imams, and act only according to what conforms to the latter, If he does so, he will be safe from the wiles of Satan. The Qur'an says: Satan has no power over those who believe and put trust in their Lord. His power is only over those who make a friend of him and those who ascribe partners to Allah. (Surah an-Nahl, 16:99)

(xxii) Daily Verbal Recitation of Liturgies

The amount and the method of the recitation of the verbal liturgies depend on what the preceptor advises. The liturgies are just like a medicine which may suit some and may not suit others. Sometimes it so happens that a spiritual traveler begins more than one liturgies of his own opinion, while one liturgy pulls him towards plurality and another towards unity. Their mutual clash nullifies the effect of both and they become totally ineffective. It may be mentioned that the permission of the preceptor is necessary only for those liturgies which everybody is not allowed to recite. There is no objection to the reciting of those liturgies for which general permission already exists.

The gnostics do not attach any importance to the mere repetition of liturgies without paying attention to their meaning which is far more important. Mere verbal repetition is of no use.

(xxiii, xxiv, xxv) Remembrance, Recollection, Evil thoughts

These three stages are of great importance for the purpose of achieving the objective. Many people who fail to reach their destination either stop at one of these stages or go astray while on their way to them. The dangers which these stages imply are idol-worship, star-worship, fire-worship and occasionally heresy, Pharaonism, claim of incarnation and identification with God, denial of being obligated to abide by religious injunctions and regarding everything lawful. We will discuss briefly all these dangers. Let us first talk about incarnation and identification with God, which is the greatest danger and is caused by devilish insinuation when the mind is not free from evil thoughts.

As the spiritual traveler is not out of the valley of ostentation, he may be led in the wake of the manifestation of Divine names or attributes to believe (God forbid) that Allah has dwelt in him. That is what is meant by incarnation, which amounts to infidelity and polytheism, while the belief in the unity of Allah nullifies every concept of pluralism, and considers every existence in comparison to the existence of Allah a mere fantasy and everything existing a mere shadow. When the spiritual traveler attains to this stage, he annihilates his existence and does not perceive anything existing except Allah.

Eradication of Devilish Insinuations

The spiritual traveler must have full control over himself so that no thought might enter his mind inadvertently and no action might be taken by him unintentionally. It is not very easy to secure the required degree of self control and that is why it is said that the eradication of insinuations is the best means of purifying the soul. When the spiritual traveler attains to this stage he in the beginning finds himself overwhelmed by evil thoughts and devilish insinuations. Strange ideas come to his mind. He often thinks of old events which have already been forgotten and visualizes imaginary events which are not possible ever to materialize. On this occasion the spiritual traveler must remain steadfast and firm, and should eradicate every noxious thought by means of remembering Allah. Whenever any evil thought may come to his mind, he should concentrate his attention on one of the names of Allah and should continue to do so till that thought has vanished. The best method of eradicating the evil thoughts is to concentrate on the Divine names. The Qur'an says: Whenever those who practice piety are troubled by an evil thought from Satan, they remember Allah and then they forthwith see the light (Surah al-A'raf, 7:201)

However, the treatise ascribed to the late Bahrul 'Ulum, does not allow this method to be adopted. This treatise lays stress on the necessity of banishing evil thoughts before beginning the acts of remembering Allah and declares it to be extremely dangerous to use these acts for the eradication of evil thoughts and insinuations. We give below a summary of the arguments advanced by the treatise and propose to contradict them subsequently.

This treatise says that: Many preceptors ask the devotees to do away with insinuations by means of remembering Allah. Obviously here remembering means mental concentration, not verbal recitation of any liturgy. But this method is very dangerous, for remembering Allah, in fact, amounts to beholding the 'Real Beloved' and to fix eyes on His beauty, which is not permissible unless eyes are shut to all others, for the sense of the dignity of the Beloved does not allow the eye that sees him to see anyone or anything else. It will be a mockery to remove eye from the Beloved again and again to see something, and a person who does that, is likely to receive a shocking blow. The Qur'an says: He who ignores the remembrances of the Beneficent, We assign to him a devil who becomes his comrade. (Surah az-Zukhruf, 43:36)

Anyhow, there is one form of remembering Allah that is allowed for the purpose of getting rid of evil thoughts. According to this form the devotee should not have the beauty of the Beloved in mind. His purpose should be only to get rid of Satan, just like the man who calls his beloved only to dismay his rival and drive him away. Thus if the devotee comes across any evil thought from which he finds it difficult to escape, he should engage himself in remembering Allah in order to get rid of that evil thought. Anyhow, the experienced gnostics ask the beginners to clear away the evil thoughts first and then to undertake the remembrance of Allah. For this purpose they ask him to fix his eyes without blinking for some time on something like a piece of stone or wood and concentrate his attention on it. It would be better if this process was continued for 40 days. Meanwhile 'A'uzu billah'; 'Astaghfirullah' and 'Ya Fa'al' should continually be chanted, especially after morning and evening prayers. After the completion of 40 days' period the devotee for some time should concentrate on his heart and should not allow any other thought to enter his mind. If any evil thought came to his mind, he should chant the words, 'Allah' and 'La mawjuda illallah; and continue to chant them till he feels somewhat enraptured. While pursuing this course he should chant a great deal 'Astaghfirullah,, 'Ya Fa'alu' and 'Ya Basitu' also. When he has attained to this stage, the devotee is allowed to resort to mental remembrance, if he wants so, in order to eradicate all evil thoughts once for all, for once the devotee has reached the stage of remembrance, recollection and contemplation, the evil thoughts and the devilish insinuations disappear automatically. This was the summary of the discourse, ascribed to Bahrul 'Ulum in the above-mentioned treatise.

Anyhow, it must be understood that this method of the eradication of evil thoughts has been derived from the method followed by the Naqshbandi, a sufi order found at some places in Turkey etc. This order has come to be known so after the name of its grand preceptor, Khwaja Bahauddin Naqshbandi.

But this is not a method approved by Akhund Mulla Husayn Quli Hamadani. Remembrance and recollection of Allah are an integral part of the method followed by him and his pupils also, but they lay greater emphasis on meditation and contemplation. We have already described meditation briefly and now propose to mention some details of its various stages.

First stage: The first stage of meditation is to abstain from everything unlawful and to perform everything obligatory. Any negligence or lethargy in this respect is not permissible.

Second stage: The devotee should intensify his meditation and try to do all that he does purely for the sake of gaining good pleasure of Allah. He should carefully refrain from all that is called pastime and fun. Once this habit has become firmly established, it will no longer be necessary for him to exert himself in this regard.

Third stage: He should believe and acknowledge that Allah is Omniscient and Omnipresent and that Allah who supervises all His creation is looking at him. This meditation should be observed at all times and in all circumstances.

Fourth stage: It is a higher degree of the third stage. At this point the devotee himself perceives that Allah is Omniscient and Omnipresent. He sees the manifestation of the Divine beauty. The Holy Prophet hinted at the third and the fourth stages of meditation when he said to his great companion Abu Zar Ghifari: "Worship Allah as if you were looking at Him, for if you do not see Him, He sees you." This tradition indicates that the degree that Allah sees the worshipper is inferior to that of the worshipper's seeing Allah. When the devotee attains to this stage, he should get rid of the evil thoughts by means of some acts of worship. The Islamic law does not allow concentration of thought on any piece of wood or stone. Suppose the devotee died while concentrating on a piece of wood or stone, what would be his answer to Allah? It is commendable from religious point of view to get rid of evil thoughts by the weapon of remembering and recollecting Allah, which is itself is an act of worship. The best and the shortest way of getting rid of evil thoughts is to concentrate on one's self. This method is allowed and approved by Islam. The Qur'an says: Believers, you have to take care of your own self.He who errs can do you no harm if you are rightly guided. (Surah al-Ma'idah, 5:105)

Concentration of thoughts on self is the method that was prescribed by Akhund Mulla Husayn Quli and has always been adopted by his pupils, who maintain that knowledge of self invariably leads to knowledge of Allah.

The chain of the teachers of gnosis goes back to Imam Ali. The number of the sufi orders which have taken part in imparting the mystic knowledge is more than 100, but the main orders are not more than 25. All these orders go back to Imam Ali. Almost all of them belong to the Sunni denomination. Only two or three of them are Shi'ite. Some of these orders are traced back through Ma'ruf Karkhi to Imam Ali Reza. But we belong to none of these orders and follow the directions of the late Akhund, who had nothing to do with these orders.

More than a hundred years ago there lived in Shustar a leading scholar and Qazi (judge) named Agha Sayyid Ali Shushtari. Like other eminent scholars his occupation was teaching and administration of justice. Many people called on him to take counsel. One day all of a sudden somebody knocked at his door. When Agha Sayyid Ali opened it he saw a weaver standing there. On inquiry as to what he wanted, he said: "The judgement given by you regarding the ownership of that particular property on the basis of the evidence produced before you was not correct. Actually that property belongs to an orphan little child and its deed is buried at such and such place. The course that is being followed by you is also wrong." Ayatulllah Shushtari said: "Do you mean to say that my judgement was wrong?" The weaver said: "What I have told you is the fact." After saying that the weaver went away. The Ayatullah began to think over who that man was and what he said. On further inquiry it was found that the said deed was actually buried at the place mentioned by the weaver, and that the witnesses produced were liars. The Ayatullah was alarmed, and said to himself: "My other judgements also might have been wrong." He was frightened. Next night the weaver again knocked at the door and said: 'The course being followed by you is not proper.' The same thing happened the third night. The weaver said: 'Do not waste time. Collect all your domestic effects and sell them out, and then set out for Najaf. Do as I have told you, and after six months wait for me in the Wadi'us Salam of Najaf. The late Shushtari left for Najaf. As soon as he arrived there he saw that the weaver in the Wadi'us Salam at sunrise, as if he had emerged suddenly from the ground. He gave some instructions and then disappeared once again. The late Shushtari entered Najaf and began to act according to the weavers instructions. At last he reached a position too high to be described.

The late Sayyid Ali Shushtari held Shaykh Murtaza Ansari in great respect and attended his lectures on theology and jurisprudence. Shaykh Murtaza Ansari also attended Sayyid Ali's lectures on moral law once a week. Following Shaykh Murtaza Ansari's death, the late Sayyid Ali assumed his teaching functions and began to give lectures from where Shaykh Murtaza Ansari had suspended them. But he did not live long and died after six months only. Anyhow, during this short period Sayyid Ali trained and guided Mulla Husayn Quli, one of Shaykh Murtaza Ansari's distinguished pupils. Mulla Husayn Quli already had some contact with Agha Sayyid Ali and from time to time used to ask him questions regarding moral and spiritual matters. When Sayyid Ali succeeded Shaykh Murtaza Ansari, he sent a message to Mulla Husayn Quli, on which he wrote:

'The course that you are following presently is faulty. Try to attain to higher positions.' At last Agha Sayyid Ali succeeded in persuading Mulla Husayn Quli to follow his method. Consequently before long Mulla Husayn Quli became a wonder of his time in morals, spiritual knowledge and self-mortification. Mulla Husayn Quli also trained some very distinguished and competent pupils, each of whom became a shining star on the sky of gnosis. His most prominent pupils included Haji Mirza Jawad Agha Malaki, Agha Sayyid Ahmad Karbalai Tehrani, Agha Sayyid Muhammad Sa'id Habbubi and Haji Shaykh Muhammad Bahari.

My preceptor was the late Haji Mirza Ali Agha Qazi who was a pupil of Agha Sayyid Ahmad Karbalai. This is the chain of my preceptors which goes back to the above mentioned weaver through the late Shushtari. Anyhow, it is not known who that weaver was and from where he acquired his gnostic knowledge.

My preceptor Agha Qazi followed the method of knowing self like Akhund Mulla Husayn Quli and for the eradication of evil thoughts and devilish insinuations he called for paying attention to self first. He suggested that for this purpose the spiritual traveler should fix a time of day or night and should concentrate his attention on self for half an hour or a little more. This daily practice will gradually invigorate his heart and eradicate the evil thoughts. At the same time he will gradually acquire the knowledge of his soul and, Allah willing, will achieve his objective. Most of those who succeed in clearing their mind from evil thoughts and ultimately receive the light of gnostic knowledge, achieve this objective in either of the following two ways: either while reading the Qur'an, their mind is suddenly diverted to the reader and it is revealed to them that the reader was really Allah; or the veils are lifted through the intercession of Imam Abu Abdillah (Imam Husayn - the grand son of the Holy Prophet of Islam), who is especially concerned with the lifting of veils and removing the barriers obstructing the way of the devotees.

There are two things which are especially helpful in receiving the light of gnostic knowledge: (i) Covering all the stages of meditation; and (ii) Concentrating attention on self. If the devotee paid full attention to secure these two things, he would gradually perceive that despite its variety the whole universe was being nurtured from one source, that is the source of all that happens in the world. Whatever perfection, excellence or beauty anything in the world possesses, it is a gift from that source. Everything has received a share of existence, beauty and grandeur according to its capacity. The generosity of the Absolute Munificent is for all, but everything existing gets its share according to its capacity and nature.

Anyway, if the spiritual traveler adheres to complete meditation and attention to self, four worlds will gradually be revealed to him:

First World - Unity of Actions: In the beginning the spiritual traveler will feel that he himself is the source of all that his tongue says, his ears hear and his hands, feet and other limbs do. He will think that he does whatever he likes. Later he will feel that he himself is the source of all that happens in the world. At the next stage he will feel that his existence is closely connected with Allah and through this relationship the favors and bounties of Allah, reach the creation. Ultimately he will perceive that Allah alone is the source of all actions and occurrences.

Second World - Unity of Attributes: This world emerges after the first world. At this stage when the spiritual traveler hears or sees anything, he feels that Allah is the source of his hearing and seeing. Later he perceives that Allah is the source of all knowledge, power, life, hearing and sight found anywhere and in any form.

Third World - Unity of Names: This world emerges after the second world. At this stage the devotee feels that the Divine attributes are not in any way separate from the Divine essence. When he sees that Allah is the Knower, he feels that his being knower is also Allah's being Knower. Similarly he thinks that his having power, his sight and his hearing are

Allah's having power, His sight and His hearing, for he is sure that on principle there is only One Being in the whole universe who is having power and who sees and hears. It is His power and His sight and His hearing that are reflected and indicated by everything existing according to its capacity.

Fourth World - Unity of Being: This world is higher than the third world. It is revealed to the spiritual traveler in consequence to the revelation of the glory of Divine Essence. He at this stage perceives that there is only One Being who is the source of all actions and attributes. At this stage his attention remains concentrated on the One Being and is not drawn to His names and attributes. He attains to this stage only when he has annihilated his transient existence completely and has passed away in Allah. It would be difficult and far from truth even to call this stage the station of Divine Essence or Divine Unity, for the Reality is far above any name that is uttered or written. No name can be given to the Divine Essence and no station of it can be imagined. Allah is even above the question of not being imagined for even negative expressions would mean that He has some limits whereas He is above all limitations. When the spiritual traveler attains to this stage, he will have annihilated his self and ego completely. He will recognize neither himself nor anyone else, He will recognize Allah alone.

While passing through each of these worlds the spiritual traveler annihilates a part of his self and ultimately annihilates himself completely.

In the first world he attains to the stage of passing away, for he realizes that he is not the source of any of his doings and that everything is from Allah. Thus he annihilates the traces of his actions.

In the second world he as the result of attributive manifestation perceives that knowledge, power and all such qualities exclusively belong to Allah. Thus he effaces the signs of his own attributes.

In the third world the spiritual traveler receives the manifestation of Divine names and perceives that Allah alone is the knower, the doer etc. Thus he effaces the signs of his names and designations also.

In the fourth world he views the manifestation of the glory of Divine Essence. As a result he entirely loses his entity and feels that there exists nothing but Allah.

The gnostics call the revelation of the glory of Divine Essence at this stage the 'griffin', which cannot be hunted. They use this word for that Absolute Being and Mere Existence which is also described as the 'Hidden Treasure' and the Being having no name nor any description.

In his poems Hafiz Shirazi has described this point in an attractive style using beautiful metaphors. At one place he says:

'An old seer and sage told me the following story, which I shall never forget: One day a pious man was going somewhere. On his way he saw a drunkard2 sitting, who said: 'Devotee, if you have some bait to offer, lay down your trap here. The devotee said:

'I have a trap but I want to catch a 'griffin'. The drunkard said:

'You can catch it only if you know where it is to be found. But its nest is not known.' 'That's right', said the devotee, 'but to be disappointed is a worse calamity.' Just see how this man did not lose heart. It is possible that the lonely man is led to the Peerless Being by a Divinely appointed guide.

Obviously it is not possible to catch the griffin when its nest is not known. But Allah can bestow His favour on the lovers of His everlasting beauty and can lead them to the world of Divine unity and passing away from self.

Notes:

1. The rightful successors of the Holy Prophet are those who have complete knowledge of Islam and who have been designated to execute his mission after him. According to a tradition accepted both by the Shi'ah and the Sunnis the Holy Prophet said: "There will be 12 Caliphs/amirs after me." (al-Bukhari, al-Sahih, al-Tirmizi, Vol. II; Abu Dawud, al-Sunan, Vol. II, Ahmad ibn Hambal, al-Musnad, vol. V, al-Hakim, al-Mubtadrak, vol II)

2. We have already explained this term.

Chapter 7

Part 3: by Ayatullah Ruhullah Khumayni - Interpretation of Surah al-Hamd

Ayatullah Ruhullah Khumayni

I have been asked to say something on the exegesis of Surah al-Hamd. The fact is that the exegesis of the Qur'an is not a thing of which we may be able to acquit ourselves well. In every period of Islamic history the top scholars including both the Sunni and the Shi'ites have compiled a large number of books on this subject. But every scholar has written his book from the angle with which he was well conversant and has interpreted only one aspect of the Qur'an. Still it cannot be said whether even that aspect has been covered fully.

During the past fourteen centuries the gnostics such as Muhyuddin ibn Arabi, Abdur Razzaq Kashani, Mulla Sultan Ali etc. have written excellent commentaries on the Qur'an and dealt well with the subject in which they had specialized. But what they have written is not the exegesis of the Qur'an. At the most it can be said that they have exposed some aspects of it. The same case is with Tantawi, Jawhari, Sayyid Qutb etc. They have compiled their exegeses in a different style, but their books are also not the exegesis of the Qur'an in every sense.

There are other interpreters of the Qur'an who do not belong to either of the above mentioned two groups. The Majma'ul Bayan by Shaykh Tabrasi is an excellent commentary and combines what the Sunni and Shi'ah authorities have said. There are so many other commentaries, but they all cover only certain aspects of the Qur'an. The Qur'an is not a book all aspects of which may be exposed by us or by anybody else. There are some Qur'anic sciences which are beyond our comprehension. We can understand only one angle or one form of the Qur'an. Others are to be explained by the Imams who were the real exponents of the Holy Prophet's teachings.

For some time past there have appeared some interpreters of the Qur'an who are totally unfit for the task. They want to attribute their own wishes and desires to the Qur'an. Surprisingly enough even some leftists and communists pretend to be partisans of the Qur'an and show interest in its interpretation. In fact they do so only to promote their evil designs. Otherwise they have nothing to do with the Qur'an; let alone its interpretation. They just want to pass their doctrines under the name of the teachings of Islam.

That is why I say that those who do not possess enough knowledge of Islam and the young men who are not fully conversant with the Islamic problems, have no right to meddle in the exposition of the Qur'an. But if they still try to misinterpret it for some ulterior motive of theirs, our youth should ignore their interpretation and pay no attention to it. Islam does not allow anybody to interpret the Qur'an according to his personal opinion or private judgement. Anybody who tries to impose his own opinion on the Qur'an is either a materialist misinterpreting the Qur'an or is one of those who give some spiritual meaning to the Qur'anic verses. Both these groups interpret the Qur'an according to their own wishes. Therefore it is necessary to keep away from both of them. As far as the Qur'an is concerned our hands are tied. Nobody is allowed to attribute his opinion to the Qur'an and claim that the Qur'an says so.

The interpretation which I am going to give is only a possible interpretation. When I explain any verse of the Qur'an, I do not claim that the verse means only what I say. I do not say anything for certain. I am hinting a possibility only.

As some gentlemen have asked me to say something on the exegesis of the Qur'an, I have decided to speak briefly once a week about the Surah al-Hamd. I would like to repeat once again that the interpretation which I give is nothing more than a possibility. I do not want at all to interpret the Qur'an according to my own opinion or wish.

It is possible that the 'bismillah' in the beginning of each surah of the Qur'an is related to the verses following it. Generally it is said that the bismillah is related to a verb understood (omitted), but probably it is related to the surah following it. For example, in the Surah al-Hamd it is related to al-Hamdu lillah. In this case the whole sentence would mean that:

With the name of Allah all praises belong to Him. Now what does a name signify. It is a mark or a sign. When man gives a name to any person or thing, that name serves as a symbol for the recognition of that person or thing. If any person is named Zayd, people can recognize him by that name.

Allah's Names are the Symbols of His Person

Whatever little information man can get about the Divine Being, he can acquire it through His names. Otherwise man has no access to His Person. Even the Holy Prophet did not have, though he was the most learned and the noblest of all human beings. No one other than Him can know Him. Man can have access only upto the Divine names.

The knowledge of the Divine names has several grades. Some of them we can comprehend. Others can be grasped only by the Holy Prophet and some of his chosen followers.

The Whole World is a Name of Allah

The whole world is a name of Allah, because the name of a thing is its sign or symbol and as all the things existing are the signs of Allah, it may be said that the whole world is His name. At the most it can be said that very few people fully understand how the existing things are the signs of Allah. Most people know only this much that nothing can come into existence automatically.

Nothing, the existence of which is only possible, can come into existence automatically.

It is intellectually clear and every body knows it intuitively that anything the existence and non-existence of which is equally possible, cannot come into existence automatically and that there must be an external force to bring it into existence. The first cause of bringing into existence all possibly existing things must be an eternal and self-existing being. If it is supposed that the imaginary upper space, and it must be imaginary because it is a non-entity, has always existed, then it possibly can neither automatically turn into anything nor anything can come into existence in it automatically. The assertion of some people that in the beginning the whole world was an infinite vacuum (anything being infinite is questionable in itself) in which subsequently appeared a sort of steam from which everything has originated, does not stand to reason, for without an external cause no new thing can appear nor can one thing change into another thing. For example, water does not freeze nor does it boil without an external cause. If its temperature remains constant and does not go below 0 degrees nor above 100 degrees it will always remain water. In short, the existence of an external cause is essential for every change. Similarly nothing the existence of which is only possible can come into existence without an external cause. These facts are self-evident truths.

All Existing Things are a Sign of Allah

This much can be easily understood by all that all existing things are a sign and a name of Allah. We can say that the whole world is Allah's name. But the case of this name is different from that of the names given to the ordinary things. For example, if we want to indicate a lamp, or a motor car to someone, we mention its name. The same thing we do in the case of man or Zayd. But evidently that is not possible in the case of the Being possessing infinite sublime qualities.

Anything Which is Finite is a Possibly Existing Thing

If an existing thing is finite, it is a possibly existing thing. As Allah's existence is infinite, He should evidently possess all sublime qualities, for if he lacked even one quality, He would become finite and as such possibly existing. The difference between a possibly existing being and an essentially existing being is that the latter is infinite and absolute in every respect. If all the sublime qualities of the essentially existing being were not infinite, that being would not be the essentially existing being and the source of all existence. All the things caused by this source of existence are endowed with the qualities possessed by the essentially existing Being, but on a smaller scale and in varying degrees. What is endowed with these qualities to the utmost possible degree is called the Grand Name or al-ism al-a'zam.

What is the Grand Name?

The Grand Name is that name or sign that is somewhat endowed with all the Divine qualities to the greatest possible degree. As compared to other existing things it possesses the Divine qualities most perfectly, though no existing thing lacks them completely, for everything has been endowed with them according to its nature and capacity. Even those material things which appear to us to be totally devoid of all knowledge and power are not really so and possess some degree of perception and knowledge.

All Existing Things Glorify Allah

As we are veiled, we cannot perceive it. but it is a fact that the sublime qualities are reflected even in the things lower than man and animals. At the most these qualities are reflected in them according to the capacity of their existence. Even the lowest creations possess the quality of perception. The Qur'an says: There is not a thing that does not praise Him, but you do not understand their praise. (Surah Bani Isra'il, 17:44)

As we are veiled and do not understand the praise of all existing things, the ancient scholars did not know that the imperfect beings also possessed perception. that is why they took this praise to mean the praise indicated by the creation of all things, but in fact this verse has nothing to do with that kind of praise, which is quite a different matter as we already know. According to a tradition once the people heard the pebbles in the Holy Prophet's hand praising Allah. They could understand the praise of the pebbles, but this praise was such that the human ears were quite unfamiliar with it. It was in the pebbles' own language, not in any human language. Hence, it is clear that the pebbles possess perception, although of course according to their existential capacity. Man who considers himself to be the source of all kinds of perception, thinks that other things are devoid of it, but that is not a fact, although it is true that man has a higher degree of it. Being veiled, we are unaware of the perception of other things and their praising Allah, and think that there is no such thing.

There are Many Things that we do not Know

There are many things about which man thinks that they do not exist, but in fact they do, though we may be unaware of them. Every day new discoveries are being made, Formerly it was believed that the plants were inanimate objects, but now it is said that they have a hearing system. If you put the tissues of a tree in hot water and pass a voice through them, there will be a reaction and you will hear some voices in response.

We do not know how far this report is correct. But it is certain that this world is full of voices and sounds. The whole world is living and is a name of Allah. You yourselves are a name of Allah. Your tongues and your hands are names of Allah.

All Movements are the Names of Allah

The praise you make of Allah is His name. When you go to the mosque after washing your feet, you go with the name of Allah. You cannot part with the name of Allah because you yourselves are His name. The beat of pulse, the throbbing of heart and the blowing of wind are all names of Allah. Perhaps that is what is meant by the names of Allah in this verse. There are many other verses in which the phrase: "With the name of Allah" has been used. As we have said, everything is the name of Allah, and the name has passed away in the named. We think that we have an independent existence, but that is not a fact. If that Being, who has brought everything into existence by means of His will and the reflection of the light of His glory withdrew His light for a moment all the existing things would be annihilated immediately and return to their pre-existing state. Allah has created the whole world by the light of His glory which is the true nature of existence and the name of Allah. The Qur'an says: Allah is the light of the heavens and the earth. Everything is illuminated by His light. Everything has appeared by dint of His light. This appearance itself is a reflection of His light. Man's appearance is also a light. Therefore man himself is a light. Animals are also a light of Allah's glory. The existence of the heavens and the earth is a light from Allah. This light has so passed away in Allah that the Qur'an has said: Allah is the light of the heavens and the earth.

It has not said that the heavens and the earth are illuminated by the light of Allah. The reason is that the heavens and the earth are a nonentity. Nothing in our world has an independent existence of its own. In other words there is nothing here that is self-existing. In fact there is no existent other than Allah, That is why the Qur'an says: With the name of Allah all praise belongs to Allah. 'With the name of Allah say: He is Allah the One'. Perhaps the Qur'an does not ask you to utter the words: 'With the name of Allah, the Compassionate, the Merciful ' It actually mentions a fact. By asking you to say so with the name of Allah, it means that your saying so is also a name of Allah. The Qur'an has said: 'Whatever there is in the heavens and the earth glorifies Him.' It has not said whoever there is in the heavens and the earth glorifies Him. That means that everything whether animate or inanimate praises and glorifies Allah, for all are a reflection of the light of His glory and it is His glory that causes all movements.

Everything in the World is A Manifestation of His Glory
The cause of all that occurs in the world is the manifestation of Allah's glory. Everything is from Him and everything returns to Him. No creature has anything of its own. If anybody claims to have anything of his own, he virtually wants to compete with the source of Divine light, while as a matter of fact even his life is not of his own. The eyes you have are not your own. The light of Divine manifestation has brought them into being. The praise of Allah that other people or we express, is a Divine name, or it is because of a Divine name. That is why the Qur'an says: With the name of Allah and praise belongs to Allah.

The Word Allah is a Comprehensive Manifestation of Divine Glory

It is a manifestation that includes all manifestations. Allah's names, Rahman (the Compassionate) and Rahim (the Merciful) are the manifestations of this manifestation.

Because of his mercy and benevolence Allah has bestowed existence in the existing things. This is itself is a show of mercy and kindness. Even the existence conferred on the harmful and obnoxious things is a show of His favor, which is common to all existing things. It is the manifestation of the glory of His name, Allah, which is a true manifestation of His glory in every sense.

Allah is a station. It is a comprehensive name, which is itself a manifestation or Divine glory in every sense. Otherwise the Divine Being has no name apart from His Essence or Person. Allah His names including Allah, Rahman, and Rahim are only the manifestations of his glory. In the 'bismillah' His names Rahman and Rahim have been added to His comprehensive name Allah, because they signify His self-sustaining attributes of mercy, favor and compassion. His attributes of retribution, anger etc. are subservient to these attributes. The praise of any kind of excellence is actually the praise of Allah. When a man eats something and says how delicious it is, he praises Allah unconsciously. When a man says about another man that he is a very fine man or that he is a great scholar or philosopher, he praises Allah because a philosopher or a scholar has nothing of his own. Whatever there is, it is a manifestation of Allah's glory. The man who understands this fact, he and his intellect are also a manifestations of Allah's glory.

No Praise is of Anyone Else's Praise

Whenever we praise anybody, we say that he has such and such good qualities. As everything belongs to Allah, the commendation of any merit of any person or a thing virtually amounts to praising Allah. We, being veiled, do not realize this truth and think that we are praising Zayd or Amr, the sunshine or the moonlight. When veil is lifted we will come to know that all praises belong to none but Allah and that everything we praise is nothing but a manifestation of Allah's glory.

The Qur'an says: Allah is the light of the heavens and the earth, In other words, every excellence and every sublime quality, wherever it may be, is attributable to Allah. He is the cause of the whole world and the whole world is a manifestation of His glory. The things we do, are not actually done by us. Addressing the Holy Prophet Allah said in the Qur'an:

You did not throw (the pebbles), when you threw (them), but Allah threw (them). (Surah al-Anfal, 8:17) Consider the words:

'You threw' and 'You did not throw.' Both of these phrases are a manifestation of 'but Allah threw.'

There is another verse that says: Those who swear allegiance to you, swear allegiance only to Allah. (Surah al-Fath,, 48:10) Being veiled as we are, we do not understand the truth these verses imply. As a matter of fact we all are under a veil except the Holy Prophet who was educated direct by Allah and the Holy Imams of the Holy Prophet's Progeny who received training from him.

So there is a possibility that the preposition 'bi' and the noun 'Ism' in 'bismillah' may be related to 'al-Hamdu; meaning, 'With the name of Allah all praises belong to Him.' It is a manifestation of the glory of Allah that draws every praise to it and does not allow any praise to be a praise of anyone other than Allah, for howsoever you may try, you will not find anyone existing other than Him. Therefore whatever praise you express, it will be a praise of Allah. It may be noted that praise is always made of positive qualities. The defects and faults being negative qualities, do not actually exist. Everything that exists has two aspects. It is positive aspect that is praised and it is always free from defects and faults.

There exists only one excellence and one beauty and that is the excellence and beauty of Allah. We should try to understand this truth. Once we are convinced of this fact, everything else will be easy. As a matter of fact it is easy to acknowledge something verbally, but it is difficult to persuade oneself to believe even a rational thing firmly.

To Believe Something Intellectually is One Thing and to be Convinced of it is Another

To be convinced of the truth of a thing is different from believing it intellectually because of the existence of some scientific arguments to prove it. The impeccability of the Prophets was due to their firm conviction. A man who is fully convinced of a truth, cannot act contrary to his conviction. If you were sure that somebody was standing near you with a drawn sword in his hand and that he would kill you if you uttered a single word against him, you would never say anything against him because your first concern was to save your life. In other words, as far as this matter was concerned, you were so to say infallible. A man who was convinced that if he slandered anybody behind his back, his backbiting would assume the shape of a dreadful animal with a long tongue stretching from the slanderer to the slandered and this animal would be crushing him, he would never indulge in backbiting anybody. If a man was sure that "slandering is the food of the dogs of hell" and the slanderer would be ceaselessly devoured by them, he would never stoop to this vice. We occasionally indulge in backbiting only because we are not fully sure of the consequences of this bad habit.

Man's Deeds Will Assume a Concrete Shape

If man was convinced that whatever deeds he performed would be embodied in the hereafter, the good deeds assuming a good shape and the bad one a bad shape, and that he would have to give an account of all that he did, he would not commit a bad deed even unconsciously. We need not go into the details of this affair. It is enough to say that everything will be reckoned. If a person slandered anyone else, he would be accountable for doing that. If anybody harassed or injured the faithful, he would go to Hell. The good men would get Paradise. One must be fully convinced and sure of this procedure. It is not enough to read the law in the books or to understand it rationally. Knowing and understanding are quite different from heart-felt conviction. By heart I mean the real heart, not an organ of the body.

Man often knows and understands a truth, but not being firmly convinced of it, does not act according to what a belief in it requires. He acts only when he gets fully and firmly convinced. It is this firm conviction that is called faith. Simply knowing a Prophet is of no use. What is beneficial is having faith in him. It is not enough to prove the existence of Allah. What is necessary is to believe in Him and to obey His commandments whole-heartedly. With the true faith, everything becomes easy.

If a man was convinced that there was a Being who was the source of this world, that man was accountable and that his death would not be his end but would only mean his shifting to a more perfect stage, he would surely be saved from all errors and slips. The question is how can he be convinced? I have already described one aspect of the verse saying: 'With the name of Allah all praises belong to Allah.' I once again emphasize that what I say is only a possibility, not a definite interpretation of the Qur'an. Anyhow, it appears that a man fully convinced that all praises belonged to Allah, could never have any polytheistic ideas in his mind, for whomsoever anybody praises, he actually praises some manifestation of Allah's glory.

Anybody who composes or intends to compose an ode in honour of the Holy Prophet or Imam Ali, that ode of his is for Allah because the Holy Prophet and the Imam are not but a great manifestation of Allah, and therefore their eulogy is the eulogy of Allah and His manifestation. A man who is convinced that all praises are due to Allah, would never indulge in bragging, boasting and self-praise. In fact man is self-conceited because he does not know himself. 'He who knows himself, knows Allah.'

A man knows Allah only when he is firmly convinced that he himself has no significance and that everything belongs to Allah only.

In fact, we neither know ourselves nor Allah. We have faith neither in ourselves nor in Him. We are neither sure that we are nothing nor that everything is Allah's. So long as we are not certain of these things, all arguments to prove the existence of Allah are of little use, and all that we do is based on egoism. All claims to leadership and chieftaincy are the result of self-conceit and personal vanity.

Self-Conceit is the Cause of All Troubles

Most of the troubles man faces are the result of his vanity and empty pride. Man loves himself and desires to be admired by others. But that is his mistake. He does not realize that he himself is nothing and that he is the property of another Being. Man's self-conceit and love of power are the cause of most of his troubles, sins and vices, which ruin him and drag him to Hell. Because of his selfishness man wants to control everything and becomes the enemy of others whom he rightly or wrongly considers to be a hindrance in his way. He knows no limits in this respect and that is the cause of all troubles, misfortunes and calamities.

All Praises Belong to Allah

It appears that the Book of Allah begins with the question that includes all questions. When Allah says: 'All praises belong to Allah', we feel that so many questions have appeared before our eyes.

The Qur'an does not say that some praises belong to Allah. That means that if somebody says to another person: 'I know that Allah is Almighty and Omnipotent, but still I am praising you, not Allah', even then his praise would go to Allah, because all praises are Allah's praises.

The Qur'an says: 'All praises belong to Allah'. This means that all kinds of praises in all conditions belong to Him. This short verse resolves many problems. This verse is enough to cleanse man's heart from the impurity of all kinds of polytheism provided he is fully convinced of its truth. He who said that he had never committed any sort of polytheism, said so because he had intuitively discovered this truth and grasped it mentally. This state of conviction cannot be secured by any argument. I do not mean that argument is of no use. It is also required. But it is only a means of understanding the question of Allah's monotheism according to one's intellectual capacity. To believe in it is the next step.

Philosophical Reasoning is not much Effective

Philosophy is a means not an end. Philosophical arguments help in understanding the problems, but they do not lead to a firm faith, which is a matter of intuition and taste. Even faith has several grades.

I hope that we will not be contented with reading and understanding the Qur'an, but will have a firm faith in every word of it, because it is the Divine Book that reforms man and wants to turn him into a being created by Allah from His 'Ism A 'zam' (grand name). Allah has gifted man with all kinds of faculties but many of his potential capabilities are dormant. The Qur'an wants to raise man from this lower position to the high position worthy of him. The Qur'an has come for this very purpose. Allah the Prophets have come to help man in getting out of the depths of selfishness and seeing the Divine light so that he may forget everything other than Allah.

May Allah bestow this favour on us also!

Chapter 8

The Difference between the Bismillah of each Surah

Ayatullah Ruhullah Khumayni

The 'bismillah' preceding one surah is different from that preceding another surah.

We were saying to which word the preposition and the noun it governs in the 'bismillah' are related. One of the possibilities is that the 'bismillah' of every surah is related to some appropriate word of that very surah; for example in the Surah al-Hamd it may be related to the word, al-Hamd. In that case 'bismillahi al-hamdu lillahi' would mean: With the name of Allah all praises belong to Allah. On the basis of this possibility 'bismillah' would signify differently in every surah, for in each surah it would be referring to a different word. If it was related to the word 'al-hamdu' in the Surah 'al-Hamd,' we would have to look for some other appropriate word, for example, in the Surah 'al-Ikhlas'. According to a rule of theology, if somebody pronounced the bismillah with some surah and then wanted to recite another surah, he would have to repeat the bismillah, and the previous bismillah would not be enough for him. This rule shows that 'bismillah' does not have the same meaning everywhere. It has a different significance with each surah, although there are some people who wrongly maintain that 'bismillah' is not the part of any surah and it is quite a separate verse revealed as a benediction. If it is accepted that 'bismillah' was related to 'al-Hamd' then 'hamd' might include everything to which the word 'hamd' applied, that is every kind of praise expressed by anybody on any occasion. Thus the verse would mean that every praise expressed is with the name of Allah, because he who expresses it is himself a name of Allah; his organs and limbs are a name of Allah and the praise he expresses is also a name of Allah. From this point of view every praise is with the name of Allah. We all are His names, or manifestations of His names, because we all are His signs, He is our originator, who has brought us into existence. The Divine

Originator is in several ways different from a natural cause or agent. One of the points of difference is that anything that is brought into existence by the Divine Originator, or in other words, anything that emerges from the Divine source disappears in that very source. To illustrate this point to some extent, let us take up an example, although this example falls too short of the relation between the Creator and the created. Anyhow, let us take up the example of the sun and its rays. The rays have no existence separate from the sun. The same is the case with the Divine Originator or the Creator. Anything coming into existence from this source depends on it for its existence as well as continuation. There is no existing being which can continue to exist if Allah withdraws from it even for an amount the light on which its existence depends. As no existing thing has any independent position, it is said to be lost in its source.

Every Possibly Existing Thing Dependson Allah for its Existence as well as Continuation

Every possibly existing being is Allah's name, His deed and a manifestation of His glory. He Himself says: Allah is the Light of the heavens and the earth (Surah an-Nur, 24:35). Every possibly existing being is a manifestation of the glory of Allah, but not Allah. Everything that appears in the world is so related to the source of its origin that it cannot have any independent existence. That is why it has been said in the Qur'an that: 'Allah is the light of the heavens and the earth.'

If it is admitted that the definite article 'al' in al-Hamdu indicated 'Comprehensiveness', the verse would mean that every praise by whomsoever it might be expressed, takes place with the name of Allah.

As he who praises Allah, is himself, one of Allah's names, it may be said that in a sense the praiser and the praised are one and the same. One is the manifestation and the other is the manifester. Some sayings of the Holy Prophet, such as: 'You are as You have praised Yourself', and 'I seek refuge from You in You', point in this direction. As the relationship between the praiser and the praised is that of passing away of the former in the latter, the former cannot claim that it is he who praises. In fact it is the 'praised' who praises Himself, for the praiser has passed in Him.

According to another possibility it may be said that the definite article in 'al-hamdu' is not for showing comprehensiveness, but it indicates that the word, 'hamd' signifies general praise without any qualification being attached to it. In this case the praise of Allah performed by us is not actually His praise. His praise is only that which He performs Himself. The reason is that Allah is the Infinite Being while all others are finite. Any praise expressed by a finite being will naturally be finite and limited and therefore it cannot be the praise of the infinite Being.

While mentioning the first alternative we said that every praise was Allah's praise. Even when you think that you are commending the merits of a beautiful handwriting, you are actually extolling Allah. Similarly when you believe that you are paying tributes to the world, in that case also you are praising none but Allah. That is why, while describing the first alternative or the first possibility, we said that every praise was that of Allah, whosoever might be the praiser, for nothing except Allah has an independent existence. Every excellence, every beauty and every perfection belongs to Him only. If Allah withdraws the manifestation of His glory, nothing would be existing any longer.

All Existing Things Are A Manifestation of Allah's Glory

The existence of everything depends on Allah's glory. While discussing above the first possibility, we pointed out that everything existing is the outcome of a divine light. Allah Himself says that He is the light of the heavens and the earth. If He takes away this light, everything is bound to disappear and come to an end. As nothing except Allah has any excellence of its own, nothing except Him is worth praising. In fact there is no excellence except His. He excels in His essence, His attributes and the state of His manifestation. All the merits attributed to anything or anyone else are His merits. Anybody who praises anyone for his excellence and merit, actually praises Him. This is true if we accept the first possibility mentioned above.

In the case of the second possibility, which is also no more than a mere guess or a possibility, the word 'al-hamdu' does not imply totality or comprehensiveness. It only signifies absolute praise without any qualification, restriction or any conception of its opposite being attached to it. But the praise that we perform is definitely not absolute. It is a particular praise expressed by a particular to a particular. We do not have access to the Absolute, nor can we perceive Him. So how can we praise Him. Even at the time of saying, 'al-hamdu lillah', you do not perceive the Absolute Truth, and as such the question of praising the Absolute does not arise.

Whatever praise is expressed, that actually is not the praise of Allah, but is the praise of some manifestation of His glory. In the case of the previous possibility no praise was that of Allah except that expressed by Himself. In this case the word 'ism' (name) in 'bismillah al-hamdu lillah' will not have the same meaning as we stated earlier when we said that everybody is Allah's name including you and me. Now the name of Allah is a symbol for His absolute and unqualified manifestation, the meaning of which can neither be explained nor grasped. It is this name of Allah that is praised and this praise can be expressed only by Allah Himself. This is a possible explanation based on the assumption that 'bismillah' is connected with 'al-hamdu lillah'. In short there are two possibilities. According to one possibility every praise is the praise of Allah and according to the other, praise of Allah is only the absolute and unqualified praise pronounced and performed by Allah Himself.

According to the first possibility there is no praise that is not of Allah; and according to the second possibility a praise can be of Allah only in its limited sense, not in its absolute sense. In this case the 'hamd' (praise) in 'al-hamdu lillah' will mean an absolute and unqualified praise. Allah can be praised only by the name that is worthy of Him. This rule is also a mere possibility.

There is another possibility that 'bismillah' might have no link with the surah following it. We know that some scholars maintain that the preposition and the noun in 'bismillah' are linked with an omitted but understood verb, 'Zahara' (appeared), meaning, existence appeared. Thus the sentence would mean:

Existence appeared with the name of Allah. In other words the name of Allah is the source of everything existing. This name of Allah is the same that is alluded to in a Prophetic tradition in the following words: 'Allah created His will Himself and created all other things through His Will.'

Here Allah's Will means 'the first manifestation of His glory' that was created by Him direct. It is this manifestation that has been called existence in the ellipsis mentioned above, namely 'Existence appeared'. On the basis of the assumption that 'bismillah' is not linked with the surah following it, some grammarians hold that some such elliptical phrase as 'We seek the help' exists before 'bismillah' These grammarians may not realize, but in fact, whoever seeks the help of Allah, he invariably seeks the help of His name. It is not possible to seek His help in any other way. Though it is not necessary to always use the words, 'with the name of Allah', the fact remains that in everything His appearance or presence is His name and thus the help of His name is invariably sought.

It is this appearance the help of which we seek and with the help of which everything is done. The grammarians may not be aware of this conception, but it is a fact that seeking help means turning to Allah. This much as to which word 'bismillah' is linked with. We said earlier that a name is the sign of the named. But there is nothing which is not the sign of Allah. Whatever you see, you will find that to be a sign of Him. Of course signs also have degrees. There are some names which are perfect signs of Him in every respect. There are some others that cannot be said to be so perfect signs. Anyhow, all existing things are His signs and manifestations in varying degrees. A tradition says: 'We are the beautiful names of Allah'. Anyhow, at the stage of manifestation the loftiest and the most splendid names of Allah are the Holy Prophet and the Imams who, unlike us who are still lying in the abyss of base desires, have reached the highest stages of spiritual journey towards Allah.

Emigration

We have not yet started even moving, but there are some people who have not only came out of the abyss but have also emigrated from that stage. The Holy Qur'an says:

He who leaves his home, emigrating for the sake of Allah and His Messenger and is then overtaken by death, shall surely to be rewarded by Allah. (Surah an-Nisa', 4:100)

According to one possible interpretation 'emigration' here might have meant going from oneself to Allah and 'home' might have meant one's lower self. In this case the whole verse would mean that there were some people who came out of the dark and dingy home of their base desires and continued to move towards Allah till they were overtaken by death, that is they passed away from self to survive in Allah, who was to reward them. In other words Allah Himself is their reward, for they attach no importance to Paradise and the bounties found therein. Their sole objective is Allah, because for a person who undertakes the path of self-annihilation and proceeds towards Allah and His Prophet, nothing is left which he could call his own. For him everything belongs to Allah. He who reaches this stage is surely to be rewarded by Allah. It may be noted that there are some who have reached their desired goal after emigration, while there are some others who though they emigrated, yet they could not reach the stage of passing away in Allah. The third category is that of the people like us who could not emigrate at all and are still groping in darkness. We are not only lost in the labyrinth of the mundane things but are also a prey to selfishness and egoism so much that we cannot see anything beyond our self-interest. We want everything for ourselves, for we think that nothing except us has any value. We have not yet thought of emigrating, because our thinking is limited to this world only.

Seventy Years Back

We do not discard the faculties with which Allah has equipped us, but we use them for mundane purposes as if we were to live in this world forever. As the time passes, we continue to get away farther and farther from the source to which we should have emigrated. According to a report once the Holy Prophet was sitting along with his companions when a loud sound of something falling was heard. The Holy Prophet's companions were startled. They enquired what had happened. According to the report the Holy Prophet said: 'A stone was rolling down in the middle of Hell. Now after 70 years it has fallen into a well located at the other end of it. This was the sound of its fall.' This event is said to be an allegorical description of a wicked man who died at the age of 70. We are all rolling down towards the same hole. I may go there at the age of 80. You will also go to that side in a few years.

Worst Enemy

It is our selfishness and egoism that are responsible for our present condition. The following maxim expresses the same truth: 'Your worst enemy is your lower self that is within you.' It is this idol which man worships most and to which he is attached most. Man cannot become godly unless he smashes this idol, because an idol and God cannot go together. An egoist can never be a devout person. We may apparently be religious, but in reality are idol-worshippers unless we get rid of our selfishness and egoism, which are the root-cause of all our troubles and evils. While offering prayers we say: 'You alone we worship and You alone we ask for help' but unfortunately all our thoughts remain concentrated on ourselves. We offer prayers to serve our own selfish interests and thus in reality worship ourselves only.

Egoism the Cause of All Quarrels

All wars in the world are due to man's egoism. Believers are not expected to fight each other. If they do, they are not believers.
A dishonest and selfish man wants to seize everything for his own benefit. It is this attitude which gives rise to all sorts of troubles. I want a position for myself; you want it for yourself. As both of us cannot occupy it at one and the same time, a quarrel is bound to arise. I want to take this chair; you also want it. When I and you want to take the same thing, naturally there will be an altercation. If two persons attempt to occupy this country, a war would ensue. All wars and battles are the outcome of selfishness, the result of the conflict of personalities and their interests. As the holy men are not selfish, they do not fight each other. Even if all

the holy men gather together at one place, there would be no fight and no quarrel among them, for whatever they do, they do for the sake of Allah. As they are neither selfish nor egoistic, they do not oppose each other.

They all have the same source and the same direction. It is we who are lying in a well that is as dark as possibly can be. This darkness is that of our egoism. So long as we do not give up our egoism, we cannot get out of this darkness. We are selfish and self-conceited. That is why we do not attach importance to others and consider ourselves alone to be all important. If a thing is advantageous to us, we accept it. If it is not, we reject it howsoever right it may be. We believe only that thing, which is in our favour. All this is egoism and selfishness. It is this attitude that is the cause of all our troubles and is responsible for all misfortunes of humanity. I want to pursue my interest and you want to pursue yours. There can be no godliness so long as selfishness persists. Then what is the remedy? Man has within himself an idol-temple. It is not easy for him to get out of it. He needs Divine help, a hidden hand which may take him out of this dungeon. The Prophets have come for this very purpose.

Aim of the Prophets

All the Prophets and the revealed Books have come only to smash this idol-temple and to take man out of it. The Prophets have come to set up a divine order in this fiendish world ruled by the Devil whom we all obey. Our base desires are the Devil's manifestation. The greatest Devil being our own appetitive soul, whatever we do become devilish. That is the reason why nothing that we do is free from selfishness. The Devil holds influence over us and we are dictated by the Devil. We can get out of this labyrinth only if we emigrate from our present stage, act according to the teachings of the Prophets and other holy men and cease to be selfish and egoistic. If we do so we will gain an inconceivable success. This emigration is essential for anybody who aspires to attain to perfection.

Major Jihad

He who wishes to get out of the dungeon of egoism, must strive to emigrate from his present state. According to a Prophetic tradition once certain companions of the Holy Prophet came back from a Jihad (holy war). The Holy Prophet said to them:

'You have returned after carrying out a minor jihad, but still owe a major one". A major jihad is carried out against one's lower self. All other jihads are subservient to this one. Any other jihad performed by us will be worth the name only if we succeed in the major jihad. Otherwise all other jihads will be nothing more than a satanic act. If a person takes part in the holy war with a view to obtain a slave girl or to provide for his livelihood, these very things would be his reward. But if a person performs jihad for the sake of Allah, then it would be Allah's responsibility to reward him. In fact the reward depends on the quality of the job performed. Obviously there is a vast difference between the quality of our performance and that of the holy men and friends of Allah, for our aims and objects are quite different from theirs.

Devotion is the Criterion

Has it been said without any reason that at the war of Ditch (Khandaq) one stroke of Imam Ali's sword was more meritorious than all the acts of worship performed by the jinn and mankind? Apparently his stroke was no more than a blow to kill a person. But it had a far greater significance. At that time Islam was facing the combined forces of infidelity and if Muslims had been defeated in that encounter, the very existence of Islam would have been endangered. There is still another aspect of the question, and that is the dedication and devotion involved in Imam Ali's act. Once while Imam Ali was on the chest of an enemy, he spat on the Imam's face. Imam Ali at once got off so that his act might not be affected by the motive of personal vengeance.

The spirit of such a stroke is certainly superior to all acts of worship. It is this spirit which gives the acts of a true believer their proper meaning and significance. Outwardly the acts performed by the polytheists and the monotheists, the idolaters and these who do not worship the idols, look alike. Apparently there is no difference in them. Abu Sufyan also used to offer prayers. Mu'awiyah was himself the Imam of Congregational prayers. They performed their religious acts like others. It is the spirit of prayer that accords sublimity to it. If the spirit is there, prayer is a devotional act. Otherwise it is nothing more than a mere show and a fraud. This principle applies to us also. We simply deceive each other.

Our Worship is For Paradise

All our devotional acts serve our own interests only. Those who are more pious among us perform them for the sake of Paradise. Take away the temptation of Paradise, then see who performs them. Imam Ali's case is different. He was in fact fond of the acts of devotion and worship. It is said about him that he loved the acts of devotion and embraced them. As a matter of principle it is not of much significance to perform acts of worship for the sake of Paradise. A person who has reached the stage of passing away in Allah, attaches no importance to Paradise. He actually does not care for it. Paradise and Hell are alike for him who has annihilated himself. He praises Allah because he believes that Allah deserves devotions. This position is attained by those who are fond of acts of worship. They worship Allah because they believe that He is fit for being worshipped.

There are many degrees of devotion. Anyhow, the first step is shunning the selfishness and getting out of the narrow hole of egoism.

For this purpose the first thing to be done is to wake up for the sake of Allah and not to remain sleeping. At present we are asleep, although apparently awake. Our waking is that of animals, not of man.

A tradition says that people are asleep; they will wake up when they will die. At that time they will realize that they were totally unconscious of the real situation. A Qur'anic verse says: 'Hell is surrounding the unbelievers'. It means that Hell is even now surrounding them but man being in a state of unconsciousness does not perceive that. When he will gain his consciousness, he will realize that there is a fire all round him. We all have to go by this path. Therefore it is better for us to wake up and walk along the 'straight path' shown to us by the Prophets.

Prophets Come to Reform Men

Reforming mankind is the mission of all Prophets. For this purpose they set up a just order. It is man who is just or unjust. To establish a just order means turning the wicked into the righteous and the unbelievers into believers. The Prophets' job is to transform the people. If people were left to do what they liked, they would certainly fall into the deep pit of hell. It is the Prophets who guide them to the right path. Alas! We are not yet following it. I am 70 years old, but am still where I was. I have not emigrated. Perhaps my condition will not change till the end of my life. Anyhow, it is essential for everybody to follow the straight path. There is no alternative.

An Appeal to the Youth

You are young and can adopt this path better. Do not worry about us, for we are already a spent force. You can purify your soul easily as you are closer to the world of divinity than we the old people. Comparatively you have detenorated less but things are becoming worse day by day. The more delay will make the matter more difficult. It is difficult for an

old man to be reformed, but a young man can be reformed quickly.
It is easier to reform thousands of young men than to reform an old man. Therefore do not postpone the task of reform to old age. Begin this work while you are still young. Follow the teachings of the Prophets. This is the starting point. The Prophets have shown us the way we should follow. While we are unaware of it, the Prophets are familiar with the way of safety and security. If you want safety, follow the way shown by them. Gradually pay less and less attention to your desires. You will not get the desired result immediately, but gradually you can get rid of your egoism. One day all our desires will come to nought. It is not in our interest to pay attention to them. Lasting is only that which relates to Allah. The Qur'an says: What is with you will come to an end, what is with Allah will remain. (Surah an-Nahl, 16:96)
Man has that 'which is with you' as well as that 'which is with Allah'. All the things that keep your attention directed to yourselves, are that 'which is with you'. All these things will vanish. But those things that keep your attention directed to Allah, are lasting and permanent.

Continue Your Effort Till You Gain Complete Victory Over Your Lower Self
You and we should make every effort to change our present state. Those who achieved success in their struggle against the unbelievers, never worried as to how many people were with them. After all it was he1 who said that even if all the Arabs were combined against him, he would not give up. As he was doing the duty assigned to him by Allah, there was no question of failure in it, what to say of being repulsed. Then there is another question. Suppose you retreat, but where will you go to? Those who advanced in the jihads, went forward without caring for their lives or their personal interests. They fought against their lower self to the utmost degree. The struggle of those who occupied a higher spiritual position was proportionately more intense. In fact man can achieve nothing unless he fights against his lower self. He cannot go forward unless he ignores his desires and keeps clear of this world, which is another name of base desires. The desires of every body are his world. It is this world which has been denounced, not the physical world.
This world is within you. When you pay attention to your lower self, you yourself become this world. Thus this world of everybody is within him. It is this world which has been condemned, not the sun, the moon or any other natural object. All the natural objects, being the signs and manifestations of Allah, have been praised.

It is this world in the above mentioned sense that deprives man from gaining proximity to Allah. May Allah grant us success in getting out of the deep dungeon of egoism. It is the friends of Allah who have gained success in being delivered from the catastrophe of egoism.

Notes:

1. Imam Ali (Peace be upon him).

Chapter 9

Relationship between Allah and His Creation

Ayatullah Ruhullah Khumayni

We were talking as to which word the word 'ism' in 'bismillah' is connected. In this regard there are several possibilities as I have mentioned.

The Creator and the Created
We cannot understand certain questions in this regard unless we know what sort of relationship there exists between Allah and the creation. We talk about this relationship either parrot-like and repeat some set words, or occasionally in addition to that advance some arguments also. A stage higher than this is the privilege of some other people. Anyhow the relationship between Allah and the creation is not of the sort that exists, for example, between father and son, that is between two things existing independently but related to each other. The sun and its rays are an example of a closer relationship. In this case also the sun and its rays are two different things, each having a separate existence to some extent. Man and his mental and physical faculties are an example of another kind of relationship. Even in this case man and his faculties are not identical, though they are closely related. Unlike all these examples, the relationship between the existing things and Allah, Who is the source of their existence, is of quite a different kind and cannot be compared to any of the relationships mentioned above. At several places in the Qur'an and the traditions the relationship between Allah and His creation has been described as Allah's glory. The Qur'an says: When his Lord revealed His glory to the mountain. (Surah al-A'raf, 7:143).
There is a sentence in the Samat Supplication which says:
'By the light of Your glory You revealed to the mountain and thus sent it down crashing...'
At another place the Qur'an says: Allah takes away the souls at the times of their death. (Surah az-Zumar, 39:42) while it is known that taking

137

away the souls is the job of the Death Angel. If somebody kills a person, in that case also it is said that he has put him to death. At another place the Qur'an says: You did not throw when you threw (the pebbles), but Allah threw. (Surah al-Anfal, 8:17) All this is the description of a light and a glory. If we ponder over this concept, certain questions occur to our mind.

Meanings of Al-Hamd

We said earlier that the first possibility about the definite article in al-Hamdu is that it might be denoting comprehensiveness. In that case hamd (praise) would mean all praises, and the word 'hamd' as well as the word, 'ism' will have a sense of multitude. From this point of view 'al-hamdu lillahi' would mean that every praise that is made is that of Allah, for it is always the praise of some aspect of His manifestation or glory. The sun manifests itself in its rays. Man is manifested in his seeing and hearing faculties. Allah manifests Himself far more clearly in every creation of His. Therefore, when anything is praised actually a manifestation of Allah's glory is praised. As all the existing things are the signs of Allah, they are His names. According to the second possibility we mentioned, the meaning would be diametrically different, and 'al-hamdu lillahi' would signify that no praise made by any praiser was that of Allah, although in this case also His glory is revealed in all the objects which are praised. But our praise cannot be absolute, nor are we capable of praising the Absolute Being.

Anyhow, as all pluralities are lost and absorbed in the unity of the Absolute Being, it may be said that from one angle even in this case it is the Absolute Being that is praised. The only difference is of the angle from which you look at this issue. If you look at it from the angle of plurality, then every praise would be that of Allah, every existing thing would be His name and every name would be different from other names. According to this possibility the meaning of bismillah will be different from its meaning according to the other possibility. The main feature of this possibility is that a sense of numerousness is implied in the conception of 'ism' or name. Allah is the name in which the stage of multitude and detail is taken into consideration. This name is the 'Exalted Name' in which Allah's glory is revealed.

Divine Glory in Everything

The glory of Allah's Exalted Name is revealed in everything. Allah's name Rahman (Beneficent) is the reflection of His beneficence in the state of action and His name Rahim (Merciful) is the reflection of His mercy in the state of action. The same applies to 'rabbil 'alamin' (Lord of the Universe), 'iyyaka na'budu' (You we worship) etc. According to the second possibility, hamd (praise) in 'al-hamdu lillah' signifies absolute and unqualified praise. In this case the conception of Allah, Rahman and Rahim will also be a little different. According to the first possibility 'ism' (name) means every existing thing with reference to its function. In other words, as the function of anything changes, it becomes a different 'ism' or name. But according to the second possibility 'hamd' in 'al-hamdu lillah' signifies unqualified and absolute 'hamd' with the names of Allah, Rahman and Rahim.

Allah alone can perform such a 'hamd' or praise and He does so with a name that is the name of the manifestation of His glory at the stage of self. In other words, He praises Himself with some of His names at this stage. Allah is the comprehensive name at the stage of self, not at the stage of manifestation. Allah's every name at this stage is His glory. Rahman (Munificent) is the name of His munificence at the stage of self. Rahim (Merciful) is the name of His mercy at the stage of self. The same is the case with such other names as Rab (Sustainer) etc. These conceptions can be proved by means of higher philosophy which is different from commonly known ordinary philosophy. But the case of the holy men, the friends of Allah is quite different. They have perceived and grasped these things by traversing the stages of spiritual journey.

Prophets' Observations and Experiences

The holy men cannot tell others what they see. Even in the Holy Qur'an many sublime truths have been mentioned in a simplified and diluted form so that they may be communicated even to the ordinary people not yet free from their low and base desires. In this respect the hands of the Holy Prophet himself were tied. He was not allowed to explain the truths to the people in clear terms and therefore he stated the truths in a weakened form. The Qur'an has many degrees of meanings and has been revealed in 70 or 70,000 layers. Having been reduced in intensity in each layer it has come to us in a form which we may be able to understand with our limited intellect.

Telling us about Himself Allah says: Will they not regard the camels how they have been created? (Surah al-Ghashiya, 88:17)

It is our bad luck that while describing lower creations like sun, sky, earth and man, the Prophets felt that there was a knot in their tongue and that they could not express the truth in clear words: O my Lord!

Open my chest for me; make the matter easy and untie the knot in my tongue. (Surah Taha, 20:25)

Other Prophets also had knots in their tongues as well as their hearts, and for that reason they could not express the truths exactly as they perceived them. They tried to a certain extent explain them to us through examples and illustrations. When an example of camel is used to explain to us the existence of Allah, it should not be difficult to understand where we stand. In fact we are no better than animals, and as such the knowledge we can obtain must be very defective.

As for the Prophets the Qur'an says at one place: And when his Lord revealed His glory to the mountain, He sent it crashing down. And Moses fell down senseless (Surah al-A'raf, 7:143). When Allah imparted special spiritual training to Moses he said to Allah: 'My lord, let me see you.' Obviously an eminent Prophet cannot ask for seeing Allah with his physical eyes. Therefore his request must have been for a kind of seeing appropriate to the seer and the object to be seen. But even this kind of seeing was not possible, Moses said to Allah: 'My Lord! Let me see you.' The answer was: 'you will not see Me.' Allah further said: 'But gaze upon the mountain.' What is meant by the mountain here? Does it signify Mount Sinai? Was it that the glory that could not be revealed to Moses, could be revealed to this mountain? If some other people had been present at the Mount Sinai at that time, could they also see the revelation of Allah's glory? The sentence, 'Gaze upon the mountain' implies a promise. Allah said: 'You cannot see Me. But gaze upon the mountain. If it stands still in its place, then you will see Me.' (Surah al-A'raf, 7:143) There is a possibility that the mountain here might have meant the remnant of egoism still left in Moses. As the result of the revelation of glory the mountain was smashed. In other words egoism of Moses was completely done away with. 'And Moses fell down senseless.' That means that Moses reached the stage of completely passing away of his human attributes.

What happened to Moses is a story for us, but for the Prophets it is an experience. This experience has been narrated to us in the form of a story because we are not yet free from egoism. The mention of the mountain or the Mount Sinai is only for our sake.

Meaning of Glory

People like us think that the glory revealed to Prophet Moses was a light seen by him. It might have been seen by others too. What a novel idea! As if it was a light that could be seen by everybody. Jibra'il (Gabriel), - the Holy Ghost used to recite the Qur'an before the Holy Prophet. Could others hear him? We do not have the slightest idea of the reality and our knowledge is confined to hearsay.

The Prophets can be compared to a person who saw a dream or witnessed something, but is unable to describe what he saw and others are also not fit to understand what he says. The same is the case with the Prophets. Neither they can describe what they see, nor can we understand what they say. No doubt the Prophets have said something, but we can understand only that which is comprehensible to us. The Qur'an contains everything. It has the rules of law as well as the stories, to the underlying idea of which we do not have access, but we can understand what they apparently mean. There are certain things in the Qur'an by which everybody can be benefited to some extent, but in the real sense the Holy Qur'an could be understood only by him to whom it was addressed. Of course those Holy men who were either trained and instructed by the Holy Prophet direct or later imbibed his teachings, also understand the Qur'an.

Through the Holy Ghost the Qur'an was revealed to the heart of the Holy Prophet. The Qur'an itself says: The Holy Ghost descended with it on your heart (Surah ash-Shu'ra, 26:193)

The Qur'an was revealed many a time and each time it was revealed in a more diluted form. The Qur'an says: We revealed it on the Night of Power. (Surah al-Qadr, 97:1). On each Night of Power the same glory is revealed, but on a reduced scale.

In short the Qur'an was revealed to the heart of the Holy Prophet many a time. It was revealed in stages, grades and layers till it finally assumed the form of words.

Nature of the Qur'an

The Holy Qur'an is not a collection of words, nor is it a thing that could be seen, heard or expressed in words. Nor is it a mode or a quality. It has been accorded an easy form for the benefit of us, who could neither hear it nor see it. Those who were really benefited by the Qur'an, were trained on different lines. Their method of deriving benefit from the Qur'an was quite different. They had a special way of attending to the source from which the Qur'an has emerged. Glory of Allah is revealed from the hidden world and reaches the physical world after having been reduced gradually in intensity. As there is a vast difference between the various grades of the hidden world and the corresponding grades of the physical world, similarly there is a vast difference between our perception and the perception of those who are superior to us and then between their perception and the perception of those who are still higher. The Prophets and the Imams enjoy the highest grade of perception. Only they can have that divine glory revealed to them which was witnessed by Prophet Musa and which is mentioned in the Qur'an when it says: When his Lord revealed His glory to the mountain. This even has been hinted at in the Samat Supplication also. The Qur'an says: When Allah revealed His glory to the mountain, a voice was heard saying: 'Moses, surely I am Allah, Each of these things is perfectly all right in itself. As for the question what should we do if we want to learn the Qur'an, it must be remembered that these things are not a subject for learning and teaching.

Exegesis of the Qur'an
If we are interested in the interpretation of the Qur'an, we have to study those commentaries which are well-known and commonly available. Some of these commentaries occasionally mention some of these subjects, but all that they say amounts to leading the blind by the blind. The Qur'an deals with all these questions, but only for him who can understand them. It has been said: 'Only he to whom it is addressed, knows the Qur'an.' This fact has been alluded to in the following verses:
The Holy Spirit descended with it on your heart. We revealed it on the Night of Power. Nobody can witness the reality of the Qur'an except the Holy Prophet, who was the first addressee of the Qur'an. Here there is no question of intellectual perception nor of any proof or argument. It is a question of witnessing the truth, not with the eye or with the mind, but with the heart, and for that matter, not an ordinary heart, but the heart of the Holy Prophet, who himself was the heart of the world. The Holy Prophet witnessed the reality of the Qur'an. As its first addressee he knew the Qur'an well. But even he expressed the truth in veiled words and by means of examples. How can we explain sunlight to a blind man? What language should we use for this purpose? Where can we find the appropriate words? All that we can say is that sight is possible in the light only. What can he who has seen the divine light tell the one who has not seen it? What can he who has a knot in his tongue tell him who has a knot in his ears. The Prophets had a knot in their tongues because their listeners lacked the capacity of understanding what they said.

The Holy Prophet's Embarrassment
This knot was causing a great deal of worry and inconvenience to the Holy Prophet who wondered to whom he should explain the Qur'an which was revealed to his heart. Perhaps there were a good number of

things which could not be told to anybody except the person who was occupying the position of absolute Wilayat. The Holy Prophet is reported to have said: 'No Prophet has been tortured so much as I have been.' If this report is correct, it might have implied among other things that the Holy Prophet was unable to convey to others what he wanted to convey. His position in this respect was that of a father keen to show the sun to his blind child. His frustration can easily be imagined. The father wants to explain the sunlight to his child, but on account of child's blindness he is unable to do so. He does not find suitable words to convey what he wants to convey.

It is said that knowledge is a great hurdle. It prevents people from undertaking gnostic journey and instead involves them into intellectual questions and scientific theories. For the Holy men knowledge is the greatest barrier and veil. The more the knowledge, the bigger hurdle it will prove. Man being egoistic and self-centred, feels elated by his limited knowledge and thinks that there is nothing beyond what he knows. Only a few persons guided by the help of Allah refrain from such false notion and silly thinking.

Tendency of Monopolization in Knowledge

Everybody thinks that knowledge is confined to what he has learnt and all achievements depend on it. The jurist holds that the only branch of knowledge that exists is jurisprudence. The gnostic thinks that there is nothing except gnosis. The philosopher is of the opinion that everything other than philosophy is useless. The engineer maintains that only engineering is important. Nowadays, it is said that knowledge is only that which can be proved by experiment and observation. Everything else is unscientific. Thus knowledge is a big hurdle. There are other hurdles too, but this is the biggest.

Knowledge, which was expected to be a beacon light and a guide has became a hurdle, an obstacle. That is true of all kinds of formal knowledge. Formal knowledge does not allow man to become what he should. It makes him egoistic. Its adverse effect on an untrained mind leads man backward. As knowledge accumulates, its disadvantages and harmful effects grow. It is no use sowing seeds in a barren soil. A barren soil and untrained mind averse to the name of Allah are alike. Some people are scared by philosophical questions, although philosophy is a branch of formal knowledge. Similarly philosophers shy of from gnosis, while the gnostics consider all formal knowledge to be an idle talk.

Formal Knowledge is a Hurdlein the Way of Remembering Allah
I do not know what we should become, but I know that our training should be such that our formal knowledge should not be a hurdle in the way of remembering Allah. This is an important question. Our pre-occupation with knowledge should not make us forget Allah. Our pride on account of our knowledge should not make us self-conceited and away from the source of all perfection. Such a pride is common among the scholars and intellectuals irrespective of the fact whether they are the scholars of medical sciences, Islamic sciences or rational sciences. If heart is not purified the emergence of such a pride is natural. It keeps man away from Allah.

How is it that the study of a book often absorbs man's entire attention, but prayer does not? I had a friend who is dead now. Whenever he forgot something and could not recollect it, he used to say: 'Let me stand up for offering prayers. I hope I'll immediately recollect it.' He thought as if while offering prayers man was not required to pay attention to Allah and was free to think of anything on the face of earth, even to try to solve any scientific question if he wanted. Knowledge which was meant to help man reaching his goal can thus prevent him from doing so. Religious law and other branches of religious knowledge are only a means, which enable us to act according to Islamic injunctions. Even action according to Islamic injunctions is not an end in itself. The real objective is to awaken our conscience so that we may be able to reach the veils of divine light after crossing the veils of darkness. According to a tradition there are 70,000 veils of divine light. The number of the veils of darkness is also stated to be the same. Further, the veils of divine light are also after all veils or screens. We have not yet come out of the veils of darkness, to say nothing of the veils of light. We are still wriggling in the veils of darkness.

As the luck would have it, the sciences whether religious or rational, have affected us adversely.

Mental and Concrete
Some of those who are wandering about in darkness call the rational sciences mental sciences. Probably what they mean is that these sciences have no concrete existence. Anyway, all sciences are a means of reaching a goal. Any science that does not serve that purpose is not fit to be called a science. Any knowledge which does not allow man to achieve the objective for which the Prophets have come, is darkness and a barrier. The Prophets came to take the people out of the darkness of this world and to

lead them to the sole source of light. They wanted man to pass away in absolute light. They want the drop of water to be mingled in the ocean and lose its existence. (It must be remembered that the simile does not represent the position fully.)

All Prophets came for this very purpose and all sciences are a means of achieving this goal. The real existence is of that Light only. We are but nonentity. All Prophets came to pull us out of all sorts of darkness and to lead us to the sole and absolute Light, the source of all existence.

Sometimes even scholastic theology becomes a hurdle and a barrier. In this branch of knowledge arguments are adduced to prove the existence of Allah, but in some cases even these arguments lead people away from Him. The method followed by scholastic theology is not that of the Prophets and the Holy men who never adduced arguments. Of course they were aware of the arguments, but did not use them, because they did not like this method of proving the existence of Allah.

Imam Husayn addressing Allah once said: 'When were You not there?' When Allah has always existed, where is the necessity of proving His existence? It is a different thing that a blind eye does not see Him.

Rising for Allah

The Qur'an mentions the first stage of rising in these words: Say: I advise you to do one thing: that you rise for Allah. (Surah Saba, 34:46)

The gnostics say that this verse describes the first stage of spiritual journey. The Manazil al-Sa'irin1 also says so. But what the verse mentions may be only a prelude, not a stage. Anyhow, what is important is that Allah through his well-beloved Prophet offers an advice and asks people to rise. This is the starting point. Those who are sleeping have been told to get up and rise for Allah only. This is the only piece of advice which we have not so far listened to. We have not yet begun walking for Allah. We do walk, but for our own sake. Those who are good and pious, are also good for their own sake only. Yes, there are some friends of Allah whose ways are different. The advice given in the verse is for us who are sleeping. Those friends of Allah have gone to the higher world. We will also be carried there. Nobody can claim that he would forever stay here. We are being pushed away by the angels controlling our organs. We will go there, but shall we go with all our veils and darknesses?

Love of the World is the Root Cause of all Troubles

Besides being the source of all things, love of the world is the main cause of all mistakes, as a well-known maxim says: 'Love of the world sometimes makes a man so irresponsible that if he feels that Allah has withdrawn something from him, he, in spite of being a believer, gets offended'.

It is said that when a person is about to die the devils who do not want him to die as a believer bring before him certain things to which he was very much attached. For example, if he was a student and loved books, the devils would bring before him his favourite books and would threaten him to set them on fire if he would not deviate from his faith. The same way the devils threaten the person who loves his child or is strongly interested in something else.

It is not correct to think that a worldly person is he who possesses wealth. One may possess a lot of wealth, but still may not be worldly. On the other hand, a student possessing only one book may be worldly if he was too much attached to it. Attachment to worldly things is the criterion of being worldly. Because of this attachment a person may become hostile to Allah when he finds himself at the time of his death forced to quit his favourite things and thus may die as an enemy of Allah. Therefore, we must lessen our attachment to worldly things. Obviously we have to quit this world one day or other. So it does not make any difference whether we are attached to the world or not.

Suppose you owned a book. Whether you were attached to it or not, it would remain with you. You could use it and could get benefited by it. Similarly if a house was yours, you could use it in every case. Therefore diminish attachment as much as you can, and if possible, give it up altogether, for it is this attachment that causes trouble. It is because of self-love that man gets attached to the world. Love of self, power and position ruins man. Love of chair and love of pulpit both show attachment to the world. All these are veils, 'some of them above others.' Instead of saying worldly people are those who possess such and such things, we should see how far we are attached to the things we possess. It is only because of this attachment that we criticize others.

A man who is not egoistic, does not criticize others. If some of us find fault with others, it is because they consider themselves to be cultured and perfect and regard others imperfect and faulty. There is a couplet which I would not recite because it is liable to some objection. Anyway, it says: 'I am just what you say, but are you what you pretend to be!'

Here in the seminary we show that we have come here for the sake of Allah. We call ourselves 'Allah's troops'. Are we really so? At least we should not pretend to be what we are not.

Is hypocrisy something else? Hypocrisy is not merely that a man pretends like Abu Sufyan to be religious while he is not so. It is also hypocrisy that a man claims to be what he is not. Anyway, hypocrisy has degrees, some of which are more severe than others. Another important thing is that when a man departs this world it should not be said about him that he was merely inviting people to the next world and was indifferent to the present one. The Prophets invited people to the next world, but in this world also they used to set up justice and fair play.

The Holy Prophet was very close to Allah, but he used to say that he sought the forgiveness of Allah seventy times every day as he felt his heart somewhat perturbed. Naturally for a man who wants always to be with his beloved, it is perturbing to meet other people and talk to them. Suppose a man came to you to ask you about a rule of law. He is a very good man, and you know that it is your duty as well as a meritorious act to answer his question, but you still feel perturbed because at that time you wanted to be with your beloved.

'Because of the perturbation of my heart I seek the forgiveness of Allah seventy times every day.' The Holy Prophet is reported to have said some such thing. But for us it would not be proper to involve ourselves in such things. At least we should be as we give ourselves out. If we have a mark of prostration on our forehead, we must not be showy in our prayers. If we profess to be pious, we must not deceive anybody, we must not take usury. Those who say that spiritual sciences make a man idler, are mistaken. The man who taught these sciences to the people and who next to the Holy Prophet knew the spiritual truths more than anybody else, according to history, took up his shovel and went out to work the same day as he pledged his allegiance to the Holy Prophet. There is no contradiction between spiritual sciences and physical work.

Those who, in order to keep people busy with their worldly affairs, prevent them from praying and saying liturgy etc., are not aware of real facts. They do not know that it is prayer that builds human character and teaches man how to live in this world respectably. The Prophets prayed and said liturgy etc. and it were they who established justice in the world and rose against the wrongdoers. Imam Husayn also did the same thing. Just see his Supplication of the Day of Arafah and ponder over it.

All their achievements were due to this prayers. It is prayers that make man attentive to Allah. If man recites them properly, then as the result of divine favour brought about by them, his self-attachment is diminished, but his efficiency is in no way affected adversely. Not only that but he becomes more active and ever ready to render service to his fellow human beings.

Some ignorant people criticize the books containing supplications. They do not know what kind of men these books build. Some of these supplications such as Munajat Sha'biniyah, Dua' Kumayl, Dua' Yawmul 'Arafah, Dua' Samat etc. have come down to us from our Imams. What kind of men do these prayers build. Those who recited the Munajat Sha'biniya, wielded the sword also.

According to reports all Imams recited Munajat Sha'biniya. I have not read anywhere about any other prayer or supplication that it was recited by all Imams. Those who recited this prayer, also fought against the unbelievers. These prayers take man out of darkness and he who comes out of darkness becomes the real man. Then he does everything for Allah's sake. If he wields the swords, he does so for the sake of Allah; if he fights, he does so for the sake of Allah and if rises, he does so for the sake of Allah. It is absolutely wrong to say that prayers make man idle and useless. Those who say such things, to them this world is everything. They believe everything beyond this world to be fantastic. But one day they will find that the things they thought to be fantastic were real and the things they thought to be real were fantastic. In fact prayers, sermons and the books like Nahjul Balaghah and Mafatihul Jinan help man in building his personality.

When one becomes a real man, he automatically begins to act according to true Islamic principles. He cultivates land, but his cultivation is for Allah. He fights but only against the infidels and wrongdoers. Such people are the monotheists and pious prayerers. Those who accompanied the Holy Prophet and the Commander of the Faithful were devoted worshippers.

Imam Ali himself used to offer prayers while fighting was going on. Fighting and praying went on side by side. Once while fighting was going on somebody asked him a question. He immediately rose and delivered a sermon. Somebody said: 'Sermon even on this occasion?' He said: 'It is for what we fight.' According to a report he added: 'We do not fight against Mu'awiyah to capture Syria. Syria has no importance to us.' The Holy Prophet and Imam Ali were not keen to conquer Syria and Iraq. They wanted to deliver the people from the oppressors and to reform them morally. It was they who were ardent worshippers. Dua' Kumayl was taught by Imam Ali to Kumayl, who himself was a warrior.

Effect of Prayer on Heart
To prevent people from praying and reciting prayer books one day some wicked people, the followers of Kasrawi etc. collected gnosis and prayer

books and set them on fire. These people did not understand what prayer was and what effect it produced on heart. They did not know that all good things in the world were due to the pious prayerers who prayed and remembered Allah. Although some people repeat their prayer simply parrot-like, yet it produces some effect, for the people who pray are better than those who do not.

A man who offers prayers, of howsoever low quality his prayers may be, is better than a man who does not offer prayers. The former is more cultured. He does not commit theft. Look at the list of the offenders and criminals. How many of them are the students of religious sciences? How many mullas drink wine, commit theft or perpetrate other crimes? It is true that the smugglers include some unreal mullas and sufi looking persons, but those wicked people neither offer prayers nor do they perform any other meritorious acts. They have assumed this disguise just to achieve their vicious ends. Among those who recite prayers and observe Islamic injunctions, there are few who have ever been charge-sheeted for any serious crime.

The world order rests on the people who pray. Praying must not be done away with. It will be wrong to divert the attention of our young men from prayer on the plea that instead of prayer the recitation of the Qur'an should be popularized. What paves the way for the Qur'an must not be given up. It is a diabolic insinuation that the Qur'an should be recited and the tradition and supplications to Allah should be abandoned.

The Qur'an Without Traditions and Prayer

Those who say that they do not want supplications, would never be able to popularize the Qur'an. Their deceptive ideas are mere devilish insinuations. The young men should consider who have rendered better service to society, those who took keen interest in traditions, supplication and liturgy or those who said that the Qur'an was enough for them. All these charitable institutions and religious endowments are the works of those who offered prayers and recited the Qur'an, not of others.

All the religious schools and hospitals were built by those members of the rich nobility of the previous era who offered prayers. This system should continue. People should be encouraged to keep their attention to the good works. Besides helping in the achievement of spiritual excellence, these prayers and supplications help in the administration of the country also. Those who attend the mosques and pray do not violate the law of the country nor do they breach the public order. This in itself is a great service to society. Society consists of individuals. Even if fifty per cent individuals in a society, being busy with prayers and supplications, did not commit crimes, it would be a happy situation! A craftsman who does his job honestly and earns his livelihood, does not commit sins. Similarly those who commit murders and robberies, are not interested in spiritual matters. If they had been interested in them, they would not have committed such crimes.

Prayers and supplications play a significant role in training society. These supplications have been taught by Allah and His Prophet. The Holy Qur'an says: Say: My Lord would not have cared for you, if you had not been calling Him. (Surah al-Furqan, 25:77)

If you read the Qur'an, you will find that Allah Himself urges people to pray to Him and says that 'He would not have cared for you if you had not been calling Him.' It appears that those who oppose supplications, do not believe even in the Qur'an. If anyone says that he does not want supplications, that means that he is neither interested in the Qur'an, nor does he believe in it. He does not know that Allah says: Call Me, I will respond to you. (Surah Ghafir, 40:60)

May Allah include us among those who are keenly interested in supplications, prayer and the Qur'an.

Notes:
1 The name of a book.

Chapter 10

Allah and His Glory

Ayatullah Ruhullah Khumayni

It is clear from what we have so far said about 'bismillah' that the 'ba' in it is not for causation, as some grammarians say. In fact in the matter of doings of Allah there is no question of cause and effect. The best way of expressing the relationship between the Creator and the created is that which is found in the Qur'an. At some places this relationship has been described as glorification: 'Your Lord revealed His glory' and at some others as 'manifestation'. It has been said about Allah that 'He is the First and the Last, the Explicit and the Implicit'. This relationship is different from that of cause and effect, which implies a sort of tendency that is not appropriate to Allah, and therefore it is not a proper expression of the relationship between Allah and the existing things.

For this purpose we have either to expand the meaning of causation to include glorification and manifestation or to say that the 'ba' in bismillah is not for causation and that 'with the name of Allah' means with His manifestation or with His glorification. Therefore Bismillah al-Hamdu lillah' does not mean that Allah's name is the cause and his praise is the effect. Anyway, as far as I remember the words, sababiyyat or 'illiyat (cause, effect, causation) are not mentioned anywhere in the Qur'an and the sunnah (traditions). These words are merely philosophical terms used by the philosophers. In this sense the Qur'an and the sunnah have used the words of Khalq (creation), Zuhur (manifestation) Tajalli (glorification) etc.

There is another aspect of bismillah. We have a report about the dot under the 'ba'. I wonder whether this report is mentioned in any authentic book. Apparently it is not. Anyway, Imam Ali is reported to have said: 'I am the dot under the 'ba' of bismillah. If this report is mentioned anywhere, it may be interpreted in the following way: The 'ba' signifies absolute manifestation. The dot signifies its first specification or determination, which lies in the state of wilayat. If this report was true, the Commander of the Faithful might have meant that as the dot determined the 'ba', similarly the state of universal 'wilayat' is the first determination of the Absolute Manifestation. The name is synonym with absolute glory. It is primarily determined by the Wilayat of the Holy Prophet, Imam Ali etc. This fact is true even if it is not mentioned in any authentic book. The first and primary determination of absolute glory is the highest stage of existence and this highest stage of existence is the same as the stage of absolute wilayat. As a matter of fact a divine name is sometimes a symbol of the state of self. The comprehensive name of this state of self is Allah. Sometimes a divine name is the symbol of the manifestation of some divine attribute such as beneficence, mercy etc. All these names are the reflections of the Exalted Name. Some of these names are the names of the state of self, some of the reflections of the glory of names and some of the reflections of the glory of doings. The names of the first category are called the state of uniqueness; the names of the second category are called the state of oneness and the names of the third category the state of will. All these are the terms used by the mystics. The last three verses of the Surah al-Hashr (59:22-24)108 perhaps hint at this division of the divine names:

(i) He is Allah, there is no other deity but He, the Knower of the invisible and the visible. He is the Beneficent, the Merciful.

(ii) He is Allah, there is no other deity but He, the Sovereign Lord, the Holy One, Peace, the Keeper of Faith, the Guardian, the Majestic, the Compeller and the Superb. Glorified be Allah from all that they ascribe as partners to Him.

(iii) He is Allah the Creator, the Shaper out of naught, the Fashioner, His are the most beautiful names. All that is in the heavens and the earth glorifies Him and He is the Mighty, the Wise.

Possibly these three verses hint at the three states of the divine names as mentioned above. The first mentions the names appropriate to the state of self. The second verse contains the names appropriate to the reflections of the glory of names. The third verse has the names suitable to the reflection of the glory of doings. Thus there are three stages of divine glorification: the stage revealing self-glory for self, the stage of revealing glory at the stage of divine names and the stage of revealing glory at the stage of manifestation. He is the First and the Last is perhaps the negation of the existence of any other being. He is the First and the Last, the Explicit and the Implicit. This shows that it is He who is manifestation, not that manifestation is from Him, for 'He is the First and the Last, the

Explicit and the Implicit.'

Glory is Not Separate From the Glorious

There are several degrees of the revealing of glory, but in no case glory is separate from the master of glory. It is an idea difficult to conceive, but once you conceive it, it is easy to believe it. It is also possible that Allah is the name of divine glory at the state of divine attributes. In this case 'ism' in bismillah will denote the revealing of overall manifestation of glory. Even in this case it will not be difficult to apply the two possibilities mentioned by us earlier, for Allah's attributes are not separate from His self or essence. In this connection it is to be pointed out that sometimes we look at an event from the point of view as to what our perception says; sometimes from the point of view as to what our intellect says; sometimes from the point of view as to what impression our heart has formed; and sometimes we witness the event at the stage of its actual reality. This rule applies to all spiritual matters.

The farthest limit of our perception is either intellectual perception or argumentative or semi-argumentative perception. We perceive things according to our intellectual capacity. In spiritual matters the lowest degree of our perception should be that we come to understand that there is Allah and His glory. As a matter of fact whatever method of perception we use, we cannot go beyond this limit.

The utmost limit of our perception is either rational perception or argumentative and semi-argumentative perception. We perceive things according to our intellect only. As far as the questions relating to the knowledge of Allah are concerned, the main stage of knowing Him is just to understand that there is Allah and His glory. In fact whatever method of perceiving Him we employ, our perception cannot go beyond this limit.

His Being And His Glory Are the Real Truth

That is the main question. As for the nature of His glory at the various stages of His essence, His attributes and His actions, the verses we have quoted above indicate only that "He is the First and the Last and He is the Explicit and the Implicit". The real truth is only that there is no existence besides Allah. In fact it is meaningless to imagine that besides Allah there can be any existence. Sometimes we calculate according to our understanding what our perception is, what our intellect says, whether our rational perception has so firmly been established in our heart that it may be named faith, and whether we have started our spiritual journey in the right direction so that it may be called irfan or gnosis. Anyhow, it is all a matter of our perception rather than that of actualities.

The Real Truth Is Nothing But He

If we look into the question deeply, we come to the conclusion that there is nothing but Allah and that His glory is not but He himself. To illustrate this truth we cannot conceive of any example which may exactly fit in with it. The simile of shadow and the thing casting shadow is defective.

The relation between Allah and His glory can best be illustrated by the example of Sea and its waves.

Perhaps this is the closest similitude. As we know, the waves of the sea are not separate from the sea itself, but still the sea is not the waves, although the waves are the sea. When the sea vibrates, the waves rise in it. At that time the sea and its waves appear to us to be separate from each other. But the waves are a temporary phenomenon. They are again merged in the sea. In fact the waves do not exist independently. This world is also like a wave. Anyhow, even this similitude is not perfect, for no similitude can properly illustrate the relation between Allah and His creation. We talk only as we perceive. There are two aspects of this question. On the one hand there are some general conceptions like the names of Allah, the names of His attributes and His actions and some stages and stations. These are the conceptions we can perceive. The second stage is that of adducing arguments to prove that Allah and His glory are not separate from each other. To prove this it is said that Allah is pure and absolute existence that can in no way be qualified or limited, for an existence qualified or incomplete in any way cannot be absolute. The absolute existence must be perfect, unlimited and free from all restrictions and deficiencies. The attributes of Absolute Existence must also be absolute and unspecified. Neither Allah's mercifulness is specified or limited nor His compassionateness nor His divinity.

Lack of Any Excellence Means Limitation

As Allah is absolute light and unqualified existence, He must automatically combine in Himself all excellences, for the lack of any excellence would mean specification and restriction. If there were a slightest deficiency or defect at the stage of His essence, the term absolute would not be applicable to Him. He would be imperfect and as such would not be self-existing, because absolute excellence and absolute perfection are essential for being self-existent.

When we think about Allah according to our imperfect mental capacity, we find that Allah is the name of that Absolute Being who has all beautiful names and attributes and who combines in Himself all excellences, and that everything else is nothing but a reflection of His glory. He is Absolute and unqualified perfection. If there were slightest deficiency in Him, He would become a possibly existing being instead of being an essentially existing Being, as He is. He combines in Himself all the excellences and meritorious qualities. He is pure and unspecified existence. Every existence is His. He is everything but in an unspecified manner and by the way of absolute perfection. As His names are not separate from His Being, the names of His attributes are also the names of His essence. All the characteristics pertaining to Allah, pertain to Rahman (Merciful) also. Rahman being absolute perfection and absolute mercy, has all the excellences of existence. The Qur'an says: Call Allah or call Rahman (Surah al-Isra', 17:110). In another verse it says: Call Him by any name, for all the beautiful names are His. (Surah al-A'raf, 7:180) Allah, Rahman, Rahim and all other names of Him are good and beautiful. Each of them combines all His attributes. He being Absolute, there is no disparity between Him and His names or between one of His names and another.

Allah's beautiful names are not like the names we give to different things for different considerations. His glory and His manifestation are not two different aspects of Him. His manifestation is exactly His glory and His glory exactly His manifestation. Even this expression is defective. Absolute existence means Absolute perfection and Absolute perfection must be absolute in every respect. Therefore, all His attributes are absolute. No disparity of any sort can be imagined between His essence and His attributes.

Observation is a Step Further than All Arguments and Proofs

It is often said: "There is no proof of such and such thing" or "Reason says so". A gnostic is reported to have said: "Wherever I went, this blind man also arrived there with his stick. By 'the blind man' this gnostic meant Abu Ali Sina (Avicenna). What he wanted to say was that the person who perceived truth by means of his arguments and cold reasoning could be compared to a blind man who found out his way by means of his stick. This gnostic meant to say: "Wherever I reached by means of my vision and gnosis, this blind man (Avicenna) also reached there rattling his stick, that is by means of his logical arguments".

People Depending On Arguments Are Blind

The people depending on arguments are blind because they lack the power of vision. Although they have proved unity of Allah and other questions relating to it by means of their arguments and have also proved that the source of Existence is Absolute Perfection, yet what they say is still a matter of arguments, behind the walls of which these people are unable to see anything. With a great deal of effort the heart perceives that the Essentially Existing Being is pure existence and that He is everything. Still the heart remains like a child who needs to be spoon-fed at every step. He who perceives the rational questions by means of arguments, need, repetition of these arguments and has to make strenuous struggle before his findings are firmly established in his heart.

Faith Means Cordial Perception

When it is cordially accepted that Allah is pure existence as well as all perfection, this conviction becomes a faith. Prior to that it was only a rational idea obtained by means of arguments. Later it produced a particular conception. When the heart accepted that conception as a truth either by means of rational arguments or through Qur'anic teachings, it became a faith. Intellect discovers the truth and teaches it to the heart. When as the result of repetition and mental exercise it is firmly established in the heart that there is nothing in this world except Allah, that idea becomes a faith or an implicit belief. Although the stage referred to in the Qur'an by the words: so that my heart may be at ease", is a stage lower than the vision of the Prophets, yet it is a stage. But the vision of the beauty of Allah is a far higher stage. Glory of Allah was revealed for Prophet Musa. The Qur'an says: When his Lord revealed His glory to the mountain. In connection with the story of Prophet Musa the periods of 30 days and 40 days and the subsequent events are significant and worth consideration. When Prophet Musa departed from the house of his father-in-law, Shu'ayb, after traversing a little distance he said to his wife: "I feel that there is a fire". His wife and children did not see at all the fire which he felt. Prophet Musa said: "I am going so that I may bring a live coal from it for you."

When he approached the fire, he heard a call saying: "Surely I am Allah." He heard this voice from the fire which was ablaze in a tree. This sort of vision was acquired by the blind man by means of his stick and the gnostic by means of his heart. But Prophet Musa had that vision with his eyes.

The Truth is Higher Than What We Say and Hear

We speak about the truths, but they are higher than what we can say about them. "Surely I am Allah". Nobody except Prophet Musa could see the Light of the divine glory that was revealed to the tree. Similarly nobody could know the nature of the revelation that was received by the Holy Prophet, Muhammad. The whole Qur'an used to be revealed to his heart at one time. How? Who knows? If the Qur'an is what we have, consisting of 30 parts, then it cannot be revealed all at once to an ordinary heart.

Heart Also Means Something Quite Different from What We Understand

In this content heart is different from what we ordinarily understand. The Qur'an is a truth and this truth is revealed to the heart. The Qur'an is a secret - a guarded secret. It must descend from its high position so that it might be revealed to the heart of the Holy Prophet. Then it must come down further so that it could be understood by others also. The same is true of man. Man is also a closed secret. From what we can see man appears to be an animal and for that matter, an animal lower than many other animals. But the distinguishing feature of this animal is that it can attain humanity and by traversing various stages of perfection can reach the stage of absolute perfection. Man before his death can become what is difficult even to imagine.

What We Feel Are Qualities and Forms

The whole man is a secret. It is difficult to say what we apparently see in this world, for we cannot perceive bodies or substances. All that we perceive are forms and qualities only. For example, our eyes see a colour. Our ears hear a sound. Our tongue feels a sensation of taste. Our hands feel the things by touching them. All these are forms and qualities. But the actual body is nowhere. When we describe a thing, we mention its length, breadth and depth. Length, breadth and depth are all forms only. We say that such and such thing has attraction. But attraction is also a quality only. Whatever qualities of a thing we may describe, they are all mere forms. Then where is the body? The body is a secret - a shadow of the divine secret. What we know is only names and qualities, otherwise everything in this world in unknown. Perhaps it is this conception a degree of which has been described by the gnostics as "invisible though apparently visible", for in this world things are visible and invisible at one and the same time. Only those things are invisible which we can neither see nor can we perceive. If we want to describe a thing we can do no more than mentioning its name, qualities and characteristics. Man cannot perceive a thing which is a shadow of the Absolute Secret, for human perception is defective. Only that man can perceive things fully who through his 'Wilayat' has attained that position where glory of Allah is fully revealed to his heart. The question of visibility and invisibility is present everywhere. That is why such expressions as the invisible world, the angelic world and the world of the intellects are on the lips of everybody.

The Holy Prophet is the Exalted Name of Allah

All the names of Allah are a secret as well as a known thing. They are implicit and explicit. That is what the following Qur'anic verse means: "He is Explicit and Implicit." What is explicit is implicit as well and what is implicit is explicit as well. That is how all the names of Allah imply all the grades of existence. Every name covers the concepts of all other names. It is not that Rahman is a name or an attribute different from Rahim. The same is true of all other names of Allah. For example Muntaqim (Avenger) is not the opposite of Rahman (Merciful).

The Qur'an says: Call Him by any name for He has all the beautiful names. All these beautiful names are of Rahman as well as of Rahim. It is not that one name means something and some other name signifies something else. Had it been so Rahman would have signified one aspect of Allah and Rahim another aspect of Him, while the Absolute Existence cannot have many aspects. The Absolute Existence as such is Rahman as well as Rahim, Nur (Light) and Allah. His being Rahman is not different from His being Rahim. A person occupying that highest position of gnosis in which his heart is enlightened by Allah Himself, not by His glory, will himself be an 'exalted name' of Allah and at the same time will be enlightened by the light of the 'exalted name'. Such a person could only be he to whose heart the Qur'an was revealed and to whom Gabriel used to come. The glory revealed to his heart comprised all glories. This person was the Holy Prophet who personally was the most exalted name of Allah. The Imams are also reported to have said: "We are the beautiful names of Allah."

Even Our Existence Is A Revelation of the Glory of Allah

The topics we have discussed today included the question of causation. We said that it was wrong to raise the question of causation in respect of Allah. In our authentic texts we do not find any mention of it. Some farfetched examples do not serve any purpose. Another question we mentioned was that of a dot under the letter 'ba'. I explained the meaning of this tradition in case it was really reported anywhere. Furthermore, some such questions were also discussed as the name at the stage of divine essence, the name at the stage of attributes, the name at the stage of the revelation of glory of action, revelation of the glory of essence to essence, revelation of the glory of essence to attributes, and revelation of the glory of essence to all existing things. When we talk of the revelation of divine glory, we say that even our existence is the revelation of glory. To illustrate this fact it may be said that if you put 100 mirrors in a place all reflecting the light of the sun, it may be said that there are one hundred lights, but actually there would be only one light reflected in all mirrors. But the light of the sun being limited, even this example is far-fetched.

All Existing Things Are the Result of Divine Glory
It is the light of Allah's glory that is being reflected in all existing things. It is the same light that is reflected everywhere. For each and every thing there is no separate light. All the existing things are the concomitant result of the same one light. As such in 'bismlllah' the ism or the name means the name of divine essence and Allah is the glory of divine essence which includes all glories. It is this comprehensive glory the name of which is Allah, as well as Rahman, Rahim etc. It is wrong to say that Rahman is the name of one divine attribute and Rahim is the name of another attribute. In fact Allah, Rahman and Rahim are the names of the same divine glory. The whole of that glory is Allah as well as Rahman and Rahim. That is the only possibility. Otherwise Allah will become a limited being, and a limited being is a possibly existing being, not an essentially existing one.

According to the details we mentioned earlier, praise (hamd) will be of Allah and Allah is the name of the Comprehensive divine glory or divine manifestation. Rahman and Rahim are also the names of exactly the same glory. Hamd means either every praise or praise in general. There are three possibilities about the name, Allah. It can either be the name of the comprehensive divine glory at the stage of essence or at the stage of attributes (This is the stage of will. Every thing is produced by it) or at the stage of action. When we apply these possibilities to the verse of 'bismillah,' a different style of expression emerges in every case. We talked about Allah on this very basis and said that it is the Comprehensive name at the stage of essence as well as at the stage of attributes and at the stage of the revelation of divine glory producing action. While discussing 'bismillah' we said a few things briefly about the letter 'ba' its dot and the names of Allah, Rahman and Rahim.

The Belief Is Essential

We hope that it will be admitted that the discussion of such problems is necessary. Some people totally deny their importance. Not only that, there are some people who do not believe in gnostic questions at all. Those who are at the stage of animals cannot understand that there is something beyond what they know. We must have belief in spiritual matters. This is the first step. The foremost thing is that man should not deny everything he does not know. Shaykh Abu Ali Sina says that anybody who denies a thing without any reason, behaves against human nature.

Belief Must Be Based On Reason

As there must be a valid reason to prove a thing, there must also be a valid reason to deny a thing. If you do not have a reason in favour or against a thing, then simply say: "I don't know". But there are some obstinate people who deny everything. As these people do not understand, they behave inhumanly. Whatever you hear you should normally admit that at least there is some possibility of its being correct. Do not reject anything outright without any reason. We do not have access to what is beyond this world. Even about this world our knowledge is defective and limited. At present we have a certain amount of knowledge. In future we will know much more. So many things which we now know, about this world, were totally unknown till a hundred years ago. In future many more discoveries will be made. When man is still unable to know and perceive this world fully, how does he dare to deny what the saints (Awliya') of Allah know and see. A man denies the spiritual truths, because his heart lacks the spiritual light. He says that spiritual truths do not exist, but does not admit that he is unaware of them. He alleges that what the believers in spiritual truths say are all fables. He dares to say so because he is ignorant. He does not know that the things he rejects as fables have been mentioned in the Qur'an too. What the Muslim gnostics say has been derived from the Qur'an and sunnah (traditions). Then how can he deny what the Qur'an confirms?

To Deny What One Does Not Know Is Unbelief

If not legally unbelief, at least it is a sort of unfaithfulness. The root-cause of man's misfortune is that he denies the truths he does not perceive. He rejects these truths because he has not reached the stage that has been reached by the 'Saints of Allah'. This is the worst kind of negationistness.

The foremost thing is that one must not deny what is contained in the Qur'an and sunnah, what is acknowledged by the Imams and what is admitted by the philosophers. If somebody has not perceived the truth himself, he should frankly admit that he does not know. But it is all humbug if some idiot says that he would not believe in Allah unless he himself has dissected Him with his sharp knife. The most important thing is that we must not deny what we have been told by the Prophets and the Imams. This is the first step. We cannot take the next step if we deny the things in the very beginning. If anybody wants to go forward he should as a first step admit that the spiritual things he does not know, may possibly he correct. Then he should pray to Allah to open for him a way that might lead him to the place where he should reach.

We Must Not Deny the Qur'an and Sunnah

If a man will not deny the Divine things and will pray to Allah, Allah will certainly help him and will gradually open the way for him.
I hope that we will not deny what is in the Qur'an and sunnah. It often happens that a man believes in the Qur'an and sunnah, and does not deny even when he does not understand what is in them, but when somebody else tells him that the Qur'an and sunnah say so, he instead of admitting his lack of knowledge, rejects that outright as nonsense.

Total Denial Is A Stumbling Block

Total denial deprives man from acknowledging many truths and prevents him from proceeding on the right path. The veracity of the facts which have been affirmed by the saints of Allah should be acknowledged at least tacitly if not expressly. A man who denies them totally and describes them as nonsense, can never succeed in proceeding further.

We Must Do Away With Negative Attitude

I hope that we will give up the negative attitude and will pray to Allah to make us familiar with the diction of the Qur'an which is of a special type. Like man the Qur'an also has many potentialities. It is a large table on which many dishes of various tastes have been placed by Allah. From it everybody can have food of his choice, provided he has not lost his appetite, which happens in the case of heart patients. The Qur'an like this world is a vast dining table. This world is also used by different people differently according to their requirements and taste. Man utilizes it in one way, animals in another and the men who are on the same level as the animals in a third way. As the level goes up, the way of utilization improves. The same is true of the Qur'an. It is for all. Everybody can be benefited by it according to his taste and choice.

Its highest beneficiary is he who is its first addressee and to whom it was revealed. "Only he knows the Qur'an to whom it was addressed."

Denial of Prophethood

We need not be disappointed. Instead we must try to be benefited by the Qur'an. For this purpose it is essential that first of all we remove from our mind the idea that there exists nothing besides physical and material problems and that the Qur'an also has been revealed only to deal with these problems and is exclusively concerned with this worldly life. This way of thinking amounts to total denial of Prophethood. In fact the Qur'an has come to make man a real human being and all this is a means to an end.

Supplications and Worship Are Means

Worship is a means. Supplications are a means. They are a means to develop real human qualities and to awaken dormant human potentialities so that man becomes a real human being, a godly man, able to see what is right and understand what is right. Prophets have come for this very purpose. Prophets are also a means. They did not come merely to set up a government. The government has its own place, but the Prophets did not come only for the sake of obtaining power and administering worldly affairs. This is what the animals also do. They also have their own world and they administer the affairs of it.

Justice Is A Quality Appropriate to Allah

Those who have an insight look at the discussion of justice as the discussion of a characteristic of Allah. The administration of divine justice is one of the functions of the Prophets. They set up a government as a means of leading man to that position which is the real aim of the Prophets' coming. May Allah help us in all affairs!

Before dealing with the remaining points perhaps it is necessary and useful to point out that the scholars often disagree because they do not understand the language of each other properly. The reason is that each group of scholars has its own language.

A Dispute About Grapes Between An Iranian, A Turk And An Arab

I wonder whether you have ever heard this story. There were three men.

One of them was an Iranian; another was a Turk and the third was an Arab. They were discussing what they should have for lunch. The Iranian said that angur would be quite suitable. The Arab said: "No, we would have inab." The Turk said: "No, I don't like either. We would have uzum." As they did not understand the language of each other, they differed. At last someone of them went out and brought grapes. Then they realized that all of them wanted the same thing.

To express the same thing there are different words in different languages. For example, the philosophers have a particular diction. They have their own terminology. Similarly the sufis have their own language. The jurists have their own terms. The poets have their own poetic diction. The Imams have their own separate style. Now we have to find out which one out of these three or four groups has a language closer to the language of those who are infallible and to the language of revelation. I do not think that any sensible person will deny that Allah exists and that He is the source and cause of all that exists. Nobody believes that you with your coat and pants are God, nor can any sensible person imagine that any man with a turban, a beard and a staff is Allah. Everybody knows that all men are creatures.

Anyhow the way in which the cause and effect are described and the impression that such description creates, often gives rise to disagreement. We should find out what those who belonged to the gnostic class actually wanted to say and what induced them to use questionable words and a vague style.

How To Reconcile Different Groups And Their Ways Of Expression?

Now I want to reconcile these different groups for they all say the same thing. I do not want to condone all philosophers or to defend all gnostics or all jurists. That is not my intention. I know that many of them are shopkeepers. They say only that which may promote their business. What I mean to say is that in all these groups there are people who are pious. The differences which exist between them are due to the scholars of to which they belong. Their differences may be compared to the difference existing between the Usulis and the Akhbaris (traditionalists). Sometimes some Akhbaris condemn the Usulis as infidels and unbelievers, and Usulis condemn the Akhbaris as ignorant. They do so despite the fact that the objective of both the groups is the same.

Now the main point of our discourse is that a group of philosophers uses such terms as the primary cause, first effect, second effect, causativeness etc. Such terms as causativeness, source and consequence are some of the favourite terms of the ancient philosophers.

Even our jurists do not refrain from using terms like causativeness and effectiveness nor have they any objection against using such words as creatorness and createdness. There is a class of the Muslim gnostics, who because of difference they have with other classes, use quite different expressions, such as manifest, manifestations, glory etc. In addition, they use certain other words to which the literalists take exception. Now let us see why they use such words and why some of these words have been used by the Imams also. I do not remember to have seen such words as illiyat, ma'luliyyat, sababiyyat and musabbibiyat (causativeness and effectiveness) being used by the Imams, but other such words as khallaqiyyat (creatorness) makhluqiyyat (createdness) tajalli (revelation of glory) zahir (manifest) and mazhar (manifestation) are found in what they have said. Now let us see why the Muslim gnostics and sufis have refrained from using the terminology of the philosophers as well as the language of the common people. They have invented a style of their own to which the literalists usually object. Let us know the reason.

Cause And Effect

On the basis of causation one thing is considered to be the cause and another to be the effect. As a rule the cause should be on the one side and the effect on the other. In other words they should be in two different places. Take the example of the sun and the sunlight. There is light in the sun, but it also emits light. The sun and its light have two separate identities and are located at two different places. As the sun emits its light, the sun is the cause and its light is its effect. But the question is whether it is possible in the case of the self-existing being also to imagine such relationship of cause and effect as is found in nature. For example, fire is the cause of heat and the sun is the cause of light. In nature the effect is a consequence of the cause and the cause and effect are usually found in two separate places.

In nature the cause and the effect are also usually located at two different places. But we cannot say about the Creator and the created that they are in two separate places or exist at two different times. Even it is difficult to say how Allah exists, because He is Absolute and His existence is abstract. Whatever the way of expression you may adopt, it is impossible to say how Allah exercises His eternal and ceaseless power of creating and sustaining every thing. The Qur'an says: He is with you wherever you are. What does "with you" mean in this verse? Is Allah by the side of every man?

Meaning of "with you"

This way of expression has been chosen because it is impossible to express the truth exactly. Therefore, words as close to the reality as possible, have to be chosen. It is very difficult to understand where the Creator is and how He is with the created. Is the relation between the Creator and the created the same as between fire and its effect? Or is the relation between them similar to the relation between soul and eyes, ears, nose and other organs? The second similitude may be closer to the reality. Anyhow it also cannot express the meaning clearly. The Creator is encompassing the whole creation and this encompassing is related to His eternal attributes of creation and sustenance. It is difficult to say anything more. All that may be added is that this encompassing is such that there is no place where Allah may not be. A tradition says: "If you were dropped to the lowest earth by means of a rope, you would find Allah even there." This is only a way of expression. For example if it is said: "All that exists is Allah". This does not mean that any particular man wearing a gown and a turban is Allah. No man who is mentally normal would ever say so. We can only use words which may be as close to the reality as possible. Only to draw the attention of a man not conversant with the reality, to the relation between the Creator and the created it is said that it is true that "All that exists is Allah". But that does not mean that any particular man or a particular thing may be called Allah. That is why the Muslim philosophers say that Allah is pure existence, and He is all things, but not anything particular out of them. This statement may appear to be somewhat contradictory. But what is meant is that Allah is free from every shortcoming. He is pure existence and has no deficiency or defect. He is characterized with every perfection, whereas all other things are defective.

Therefore He 'is not anything particular out of them'. As Allah is free from every defect and deficiency, He consequently enjoys every perfection. Any perfection found in any creation of His is a reflection of His own perfection. As every perfection is a revelation of His glory, He Himself is all perfection. In the above quoted tradition "all things" means all kinds of perfection and "not anything particular out of them" means that He is free from every defect and deficiency. "All things" does not mean that you are also Allah.

That is why it is said that "He is not any thing particular out of them." In other words He is all perfection while no one else is characterized with every perfection. There is another example of this kind. There is a well-known Persian poetical line that means: 'Because non-attachment became confined to attachment.' This line has nothing to do with any question of divinity. But those who are not conversant with this topic, often confuse its meaning. This line in fact is concerned with the hostility between two persons. But those who do not understand its meaning say that it amounts to infidelity. In fact it has been misunderstood and misinterpreted. It actually deals with quite a different question, that is why the wars occur in the world.

Why Do the Wars Occur?
Why are the wars fought? What is the basis of the wars? In the above mentioned line and in Persian the word, 'rung' (colour) is used in the sense of attachment and 'berungi' (colourlessness) in the sense of non-attachment. Some other poets have also used these words in this sense.

If one is not attached to any thing, there can be no quarrel. All quarrels are caused by somebody's attachment to some thing, which he wants to obtain for himself. The poet who wrote the above mentioned line wants to say that attachment to any particular thing or things is not a part of real human nature and if this attachment to worldly things is done away with there will no longer be any quarrel.

In the story of Prophet Musa and Fir'awn, if Fir'awn had been as indifferent to worldly things as Prophet Musa was, there would have been no trouble. If all the Prophets gathered together at a place there would be no dispute at all, for all disputes and quarrels are due to attachment. Nature was unattached, but when it became a captive of attachment, quarrels arose. Even Prophet Musa and Fir'awn would make friends, if the sting of attachment was removed. This topic has no concern with divinity. It did not occur to him who objected to this line, that it related to two men quarreling between themselves.

Words in Imam's Supplications
You are already familiar with the words used in Imams' supplications. Now let us see whether the words and phrases used by Muslim gnostics for which they have been charged with unbelief by those who are unaware of reality, are similar to those used by the Imams or the gnostics have a different vocabulary. This topic relates to spiritual journey.

The following words have come in the Sha'baniyah supplication:

"O my Lord! Grant me complete withdrawal to You and enlighten the eyes of our heart with the light of looking towards You so that the eyes of heart may tear off the curtains of light and reach the source of granduer and our souls get suspended in the honourable chamber of your sanctity."

Further the text says: "O my Lord! Grant me that I may be one of those whom you called and they responded, and at whom You looked and they were dumb-founded."

What do these words signify? Now what do the critics of the gnostics say? The gnostics have not said anything different from what the Imams have said. Why did all our Imams use to recite this supplication? What does "complete withdrawal" mean?

Imams pray for complete withdrawal

The Imams ask Allah to grant them complete withdrawal to Him, while it was up to them to undertake the spiritual journey themselves, but still they prayed to Allah for it. Why so? They asked Allah to enlighten the eyes of their hearts. What did they mean by the eyes of the hearts with which they wished to see Allah? What does heart mean in this context, and what is the meaning of the eye of the heart? Thereafter, the aim of all this has been stated in these words: "So that the eyes of our heart may tear off the curtains of light and may reach the source of majesty and our souls may become suspended in the honourable chamber of Your sanctity". Here the question arises what is meant by becoming suspended? The next prayer is:

"O my Lord! Make me one of those whom you called and who responded to You and who were dumbfounded by Your majesty." The Qur'an also has said about Prophet Musa that he fell down senseless. Are these expressions different from what is called fana' or passing away in the terminology of the Muslim gnostics. Thus climbing up higher and higher the spiritual traveller reaches the stage where the eyes of his heart tearing off all curtains reach the source of majesty. What is this source of majesty and what does reaching this source mean? Does this not mean gaining that proximity to Allah of which the gnostics talk? Can anything other than Allah be the source of majesty? Only that can be this source of majesty from whom all the favours and blessings can be contained. Only after reaching this source of majesty "our souls will become suspended in the honourable chamber of Your sanctity".

Anybody who looks over the relationship between Allah and His creation will never use the words, cause and effect for this relationship. The use of these words, wherever it has been made, shows only that this relationship is such that it cannot be expressed in exact terms. The use of the words Creator and creation is nothing but following the taste of the common people. A far better expression is revealing the glory. The Qur'an says: Then his Lord revealed His glory to the mountain. (Surah al-A'raf, 7:143) This is also only a way of using the closest words to state a relationship that cannot be expressed exactly.

A Question Difficult To Conceive, But Easy to Believe

The relationship between Allah and His creation is a question that is difficult to conceive but after having been conceived, is easy to be believed. The difficulty is how to conceive a Being who is everywhere, but still it cannot be said that He is at such and such place. He is outside of everything as well as the inside of everything. Everything is caused by Him. Nothing is devoid of Him. Now where can we find appropriate words to express these concepts? Whatever words we choose, they will be inadequate. All that can be done is that those who are fit to do so pray to Allah and pray in the style of the Shabaniyah Supplication that He may enlighten them on this subject. Anyhow, it is not a thing for which one group may declare another group infidel or ignorant, for it is not possible for anyone to express himself clearly on this subject. Try to understand the sentiments of others and what they want to say. Sometimes it happens that as light surges in the heart of somebody, he involuntarily exclaims that he is everything.

Imam Ali is the Eye of Allah, He is the Light of Allah's Eye

You read in the supplications that Imam Ali is the eye of Allah. What does that signify? Imam Ali is often described as the eye of Allah, light of Allah and the hand of Allah. What does the Hand of Allah mean? Such words are used by the Muslim gnostics also. It is reported in our traditions that the alms given to a poor-man reaches the Hand of Allah.

The Qur'an says: You did not throw the pebbles, when you threw them, but Allah threw. (Surah al-Anfal, 8:17) What does this mean? This is what you all repeat, but you do not allow the gnostics to mention the Hand of Allah. When these poor people cannot say expressly, they say the same thing in a roundabout way. But such expressions are common even in the Qur'an and especially in the Imams' supplications. Therefore there is no reason why we should suspect the gnostics especially. Try to understand what they mean and why they do not use the diction commonly used by other people. Although they have not used the familiar words and phrases, they have not sacrificed the truth, but have sacrificed themselves for the sake of truth. If we could understand that truth, we might have used the same diction.

The Qur'an has used the same way of expression. The Imams also have used similar words. If somebody says: "This is the truth", no sensible person will think that he means that this is Allah. Now just see how manifestation of Allah can be interpreted? In regard to the Imams in a supplication the following words have been used: "There is no difference between You and them, except that they are your bondsmen; their creation is in Your Hand and their restoration is in Your Hand." This sentence also shows the inadequacy of expression. That is why the Imams use the words which are closer to the Qur'an than to the words used by others.

About gnostics anyone could say that they were nobody. But there were some other people whom we knew intimately and knew that they had a thorough knowledge of all Islamic sciences. They also used similar words. For example they used to say: "That reveals Allah's glory". In the 'Samat' Supplication there is a word, 'tal'atuka'. This word also means glory. Similarly there is another word nur (light) in the phrase, 'binuri wajhika' (by the light of Your Countenance). That is why I say: Make peace with the gnostics. I do not mean to say that all of them are good. What I mean is that all of them must not be rejected. When I support the scholars and jurists, I do not intend to support all kinds of scholars and what I mean is that all of them should not be rejected. The same is the case with the gnostics. Do not think that whosoever talks in gnostic terms is an infidel.

Every Thing Must Be Investigated
First of all it must be understood what the other man is saying. If that is understood, perhaps there will be no need of rejecting him. Everywhere it is the same story of grapes – 'inab, angur and uzum.' One man states a thing in one way; another man uses the terms of cause and effect while saying the same thing; the third man uses the word, mover and consequence; while the fourth man says manifest and manifestation. At some time or other all of them reach a stage where they realize how to describe the Being who is everywhere but is not any of the things we perceive. That is why sometimes someone ever says:
"Ali is Allah's hand; Ali is Allah's eye."
The Qur'an says: You did not throw when you threw, but Allah threw. It also says: Surely those who pledge their allegiance to you, really pledge their allegiance to Allah. Allah's hand is above their hands. (Surah al-Fath, 48:10)
Does this verse mean that Allah's Hand is literally placed on their

hands? Obviously it does not. 'Above' here means at a higher point spiritually. Actually we lack words to express this position properly.

As Allah is far above that he may be mingled with anything or that he may be related to anything in a general sense, similarly he is above that we may be able to understand the nature of His glory. His glory is unknown to us. But we believe that there is certainly something of this sort. We cannot deny its existence. When we believe that such things exist, we have to admit that they are mentioned in one way or another in the Qur'an and Sunnah. In the Qur'an wherever there is a mention of the glory of Allah, the words revealing or manifesting have been used. In the Surah al-Hadid a verse says: He is Explicit and Implicit.

A report says that the last six verses of the Surah al-Hadid are for the people who will appear "in the last era." Only they will be able to understand these verses which give some account of creation etc. It is in these verses that Allah says: He is the First and the Last and the Explicit and the Implicit and He is with you wherever you are. (Surah al-Hadid, 57:3-4) Nobody can easily understand what is meant by 'the last era'. Only one or two persons in the world may be able to understand the significance of this phrase.

Misunderstandings Must Be Removed

The main point which I want to emphasize is that misunderstanding must be removed and there should be an end to the differences between the pedagogues and the scholars. The way to gnosis must not be blocked. Islam is not the name of the rules of law only. The basis of these rules is something else. The basis should not be considered to be superfluous, nor should it be sacrificed for the sake of derivatives. We must not say that gnosis is not required or has no importance. Someone told me that a person was mentioned before the late Shaykh Muhammad Bahari. He says: "That man is a righteous infidel." 'How can that be' we said: 'Is he righteous and at the same time an infidel?' Shaykh Muhammad Bahari said: 'Yes, he is righteous because he acts according to the law of Islam and does not commit any sin. And he is an infidel because the god which he worships is not true God.'

Even the Ant Loves Itself

According to our traditions perhaps the ant thinks that Allah has two horns. This is due to self-love which an ant also apparently harbours. The ant is a very funny creature. It thinks that it is a mark of granduer to have horns. When we think about our virtues and merits, we also think almost in the same way. It is the same ant which thought that Prophet Sulayman (Soloman) and his troop could not understand anything. The Qur'an says:

An ant exclaimed: 'O ants: Enter your dwellings lest Sulayman and his troops crush you because they do not understand.' 'And he (Sulayman) smiled laughing at her speech. (Surah an-Naml, 27:17-19)

The case of the ant is not a solitary one. Everybody thinks the same way. Even the hoopoe, according to the Qur'an, said:

I know what you do not. (Surah an-Naml, 27:22). The hoopoe said so to Prophet Sulayman who was a Prophet and who had a companion who brought to him the throne of Bilqis in the twinkling of an eye. How could he do that, is not known. Was there any electric system of transportation, or was it a case of annihilating a thing and then bringing it back into existence, or was the throne of Bilqis transported after having been converted into electric waves? According to a report one of the companions of Prophet Sulayman knew a letter of Allah's Exalted Name and by virtue of it could bring anything desired to Prophet Sulayman before the twinkling of an eye. To such a prophet the hoopoe said: 'I know what you do not.'

Anyway, what Shaykh Muhammad Bahari meant to say was that that particular scholar said what he understood and he acted also accordingly.

It Is Bad Luck To Be Unaware of Some Important Questions

I think that it is unfortunate that a group of scholars which includes some very good and pious persons, is unaware of some important questions. When I came to Qum, Mirza Ali Akbar Hakim was there. He had established an Islamic Academy at his house. The scholars used to receive education there. Such outstanding persons as the late Agha Khawansari and the late Agha Ishraqi used to attend Mirza Ali Akbar's lectures. On that occasion a pious and prominent personality, who is no longer amongst us, remarked: 'Look, to what level has the condition of Islam gone down? Now the business of Islam is being transacted at the house of Mirza Ali Akbar.' He made this remark despite the fact that personally he was a pious man. Even after his death one of his representatives said on the pulpit: 'I have myself seen Mirza Ali Akbar reciting the Qur'an.' The late Agha Shah Abadi was very much offended by this remark. Such misunderstandings are regrettable, and keeping oneself aloof from good work is also deplorable. What a pity that this scholar did not take part in the meritorious act of setting up a learned academy!

Philosophy is a common place thing, but some people object to it also. In fact these people do not understand each other and that is why all the disputes arise. A scholar declares another scholar infidel simply because he does not understand what the other man says. The fault of the other man is that he uses such terms as cause, effect etc., which in the eyes of the former are contrary to the facts. I said earlier that divine name is not separate from the named. The name is a manifestation and a sign, but not such a sign as a milestone is. Therefore it is difficult to say that such and such thing is a sign of Allah. The words used in the Qur'an are closest to the reality but still do not represent it fully. The difficulty is that better words do not exist.

I said earlier that the Qur'an was like a dining table with many dishes placed on it. Everybody can have food according to his choice. No group has a monopoly of the Qur'an. All have a right to be benefited by it equally. The supplications of the Imams are full of spiritual knowledge. But some individuals try to deprive the people of these supplications which impart knowledge and convey the views of the Qur'an. Imams' supplications interpret the Qur'an and explain the questions to which others do not have access.

It is Wrong To Persuade People To Give Up Supplications
It is wrong to say that as we want to concentrate on the Qur'an, the supplications are not required. People should cultivate a liking for the supplications so that they may develop an attachment to Allah. Those who do so, give no importance to worldly things. They are not self-conceited, and keep them-
selves busy with the tasks liked by Allah. Such people include those who used to fight for the sake of Allah, and at the same time used to recite the supplications. Their circumstances were not different from ours, but still they managed to wield the sword and pray at the same time. Just as the Holy Prophet and the Holy Qur'an are not separate from each other, similarly the Holy Qur'an and the supplications are also not separate from each other.

We cannot say that as we have the Qur'an, we do not need the Holy Prophet. The Qur'an and the Holy Prophet go together. "They will always remain together till they arrive together at the Fountain of Kawthar." There is no question of their parting.

If some of us take them separately and want the Qur'an to be separate, the Imams to be separate and the supplications to be separate; or if some of us say that the books of supplication are not required, and as such they may be set on fire; or if some of us want the books of the gnostics to be burnt, the reason is simply that the people who say and do such thing are ignorant. A man who exceeds his limit always falls into error.

Kasrawi And Hafiz

Kasrawi was an historian. His knowledge of history was good. He was a fine writer also. But he was self conceited. In the end he began to claim to be a prophet. He, however, believed in the Qur'an, but he was totally against supplications. He lowered Prophethood and brought it down to his own level. As he himself could not rise up, he lowered Prophethood. The supplications and the Qur'an all go together. The gnostics, the sufi poets and the philosophers all say the same thing. Their points of view are not different. The difference is only that of their diction and the style of expression. Hafiz Shirazi (the Celebrated Persian Poet) has his own individual style. He mentions the same points as others do, but in a different manner. Their choice of words may be different, but the people should not be deprived of the blessings of the subject matter. It is essential to call people to the vast treasure of knowledge contained in the Qur'an, sunnah and supplications so that everybody may be benefited by them according to his capacity.

This was a prelude to the points I intend to put forward later. If I am spared and mention any expression used by the gnostics as a possibility, it should not be said that I was trying to revive their expressions. In fact their expressions are worth being popularized. Some craftsmen used to call on the late Agha Shah Abadi, who used to narrate gnostic problems in front of them as in front of others. One day I said: 'Do you narrate these things in front of these people also?' He said: 'Never mind! Let these heresies be heard by them too'.

We also had some such people. I cannot say who they were. It will be wrong to mention anybody by name. Now the topic of discussion is that "Bismillahir Rahmanir Rahim" has al-Rahman al-Rahim and "Al-hamdu lillahi Rabbil 'alamin" is also followed by the same words, viz. al-Rahman al-Rahim. The words al-Rahman and al-Rahi'm may in bismillah either relate to ism or Allah. Both the possibilities are there. God-willing we will see later which of these two possibilities appears to be more reasonable.

Chapter 11

Appendix: The Invocation of Shabaniyah

My Lord, bestow Your blessings on Muhammad and his descendants; respond to my prayer when I pray to You; listen to my call when I call You; and turn to me when I make my submission to You in confidence. I have come running to You and am standing before You imploring You in humility and hoping to get the reward You have for me. You know what is in my heart, and You are aware of what I need. You know my mind and are not unaware of my future and of my present, of what I want to begin my speech with; of the request I would utter, and of the hopes I have in regard to my ultimate lot.

My Lord, whatever You have destined for me up to tbe end of my life, whether concerning the open aspect of my life or the hidden aspect of it, is bound to come. What is to my advantage and what is to my disadvantage - all my losses and gains are in Your hand, not in the hand of anybody else.

My Lord, if You deprive me, who else will provide me; and if You let me down, who else will help me?

My Lord, I seek Your protection from Your anger and from earning Your displeasure. If I am not fit for gaining Your Mercy, You are certainly fit to be generous to me by virtue of Your Magnanimity.

My Lord, I see as if I am standing before You protected by my trust in You. You said what befitted You and covered me with Your forgiveness.

My Lord, if You forgive me, then who is more suited than You to do that? If the time of my death has come near and my deeds have not still brought me close to You, I make this confession of my sins a means of approaching You. I have been unjust to my soul for I have not looked after it. It will certainly be doomed if You do not forgive it.

My Lord, You have always been kind to me during my life time. Therefore do not cut off Your favour from me at the time of my death.

My Lord, how can lose the hope of Your looking kindly, in me after my death, when you have always been good to me during my life.

My Lord, in my case do what befits You and bestow Your favour on me - a sinner enwrapped in his ignorance.

My Lord, You have concealed many of my sins in this world. I am in a greater need of their being conceded in the next. As You have not revealed my sins even to any of Your pious bondmen, do not expose me on the Day of Resurrection before everybody.

My Lord, Your generosity has expanded my aspiration, and Your forgiveness is superior to my deeds. Therefore gladden my heart by allowing me to meet You on the day You adminis-ter justice to Your bondmen.

My Lord, my apology to You is the apology of him who cannot afford his apology being not accepted. Therefore accept my apology, You the Most Magnanimous of those to whom the evildoers tender their apology.

My Lord, do not turn down my request; do not foil my desire; and do not cut off my hope and expectation of You.

My Lord, if You had wanted to disgrace me, You would not have guided me; and if You had wanted to expose my faults and vices, You would not have kept me safe and sound.

My Lord, I do not think that You will turn down my request for that in asking You for which I have spent my whole life.

My Lord, all praise is due to You, always and forever, growing not diminishing, as You like and please.

My Lord, if You condemn me for my crimes, I will cling to Your forgiveness, and if You hold me for my sins, I will cling to Your granting pardon. If You haul me into the hell, I will tell its inmates that I love You.

My Lord, if my deeds are too small in relation to how I should obey You, my aspirations are high enough as compared to what I should expect of You.

My Lord, how can I go away from You unsuccessful and disappointed, when I had a high hope that You will be kind enough to send me away enjoying safety and deliverance.

My Lord, I have wasted my life committing the crime of forgetting You and played havoc with my youth, intoxicated with keeping myself away from You.

My Lord, I did not wake up when I was under a delusion about You and was inclined to earn Your displeasure.

My Lord, I am Your bondman, son of Your bondman. I am standing before You, trying to use Your own magnanimity as a means of approaching You.

My Lord, I am a bondman of Yours, I want to rid myself of the sins I used to commit in Your presence because I lacked the sense of feeling ashamed that You were looking at me. I request You to forgive me, be-cause forgiveness is a character-istic of Your Kindness.

My Lord, I was not strong enough to move away from Your disobedi-ence, except when You awakened me to Your love. I was exactly as You wanted me to be. I am thankful to You for introducing me to Your Kind-ness and purging my heart of the impurities of being inattentive to You.

My Lord, look upon me as the person whom You called and he respon-ded to You, whom You helped by using his ser-vices, and he obeyed You. You Near One, Who is not far from one who is away from You. You Munificent, Who does not withhold His reward from one who hopes for it.

My Lord, provide me with a heart, the passion of which may bring it near You, with a tongue the truth of which may be submitted to You, and with a vision the nature of which may bring it close to You.

My Lord, whoever gets acquainted with You, is not un-known; whoever takes shelter under You, is not disappointed; and one to whom You turn, is not a slave. One who follows Your path is enlightened; and one who takes refuge in You, is saved.

My Lord, I have taken refuge in You. Therefore do not disappoint me of Your Mercy and do not keep me secluded from Your Kindness.

My Lord, place me among Your friends in the position of one who hopes for an increase in Your love.

My Lord, inspire me with a passionate love of remember-ing You so that I may keep on remembering You, and by Your Holy Name and Pure Position cherish my cheerful determination into a success.

My Lord, I invoke You to admit me to the place reserved for those who obey You, and to attach me to the nice abode of those who enjoy Your good pleasure... I can neither defend myself nor do I control what is ad-vantageous for me.

My Lord, I am Your powerless sinning slave and Your repentant bond-man. So do not make me one of those from whom You turn away Your face, and whom his negligence has secluded from Your forgiveness.

My Lord, grant me complete severance of my relations with everything else and total submission to You. Enlighten the eyes of our hearts with the light of their looking at You to the extent that they penetrate the veils of light and reach the Source of Grandeur, and let our souls get suspen-ded by the glory of Your sanctity.

My Lord, make me one of those whom You call and they respond; when You look at and they are thunderstruck by Your majesty. You whisper to them secretly and they work for You openly.

My Lord, I have not allowed my pessimistic despair to overcome my good opinion about You, nor did I ever lose my hope of Your benevolence.

My Lord, if my errors have degraded me with You, You may forgive me in view of my unqualified reliance on You.

My Lord, if my sins have made me unfit to receive Your tender affection, my firm belief has reminded me of Your Compassion.

My Lord, if my disregard for preparations to meet You has put me to sleep, my knowledge of Your kind bounties has awakened me.

My Lord, if Your severe punishment calls me to Hell, the abundance of Your reward invites me to Paradise.

My Lord, I ask You and pray to You earnestly, I desire and request You to show Your favour to Muhammad and his descendants, make me one of those who always remember You and never violate the pledge they make to You, who do not fail to show You their gratitude and do not take Your orders lightly.

My Lord, let me be attached to the Light of Your Majestic Glory, so that I may know You alone, be away from others, and have a heart fearful of You and an eye watchful of You. May Allah's blessing and peace be on Muhammad and those of his descendants who are pure.

From the same author on Feedbooks

Woman And Her Rights *(2012)*
Social independence of women, modern life and Islam, women in
Qur'an, family rights, differences between men and women, inher-
itance, divorce, mut'a, and polygamy is discussed in this book by
Ayatullah Murtada Mutahhari.
A translation of Nizam-e-Huqooq-e-Zan dar Islam by M A Ansari
Published by the Islamic Seminary Publications
Thanks to al-islam.org
islamicmobility.com

Spiritual Discourses *(2012)*
Criteria for humanity, spiritual freedom, nobility, worship and
prayer, repentance, migration, jihad, and belief in the unseen.
al-islam.org - islamicmobility.com
Translated by Dr. Aluddin Pazargadi
Edited by Salman Tawhidi
Published by: Islamic Propagation Org Tehran

IslamicMobility.com
In the age of Information
Ignorance is a choice

"Wisdom is the lost property of the Believer,

let him claim it wherever he finds it"

Imam Ali (as)

30288567R00101

Made in the USA
Lexington, KY
08 February 2019